DRAWING THE

BIG RED MACHINE

BASEBALL'S GREATEST TEAM

MORE THAN 300 DRAWINGS BY

JERRY DOWLING

FOREWORD BY

BASEBALL'S GREATEST CATCHER

JOHNNY BENCH

HALL OF FAME '89

AFTERWORD BY

BOB QUINN

GENERAL MANAGER, 1990 WORLD CHAMPION REDS

TO BILL SYMONDS —
I WISH I COULD HIT 'EM, —
'FIELD 'EM — RUN AS
WELL AS YOU! BEST ALWAYS!
YOUR FRIEND
Jerry Dowling

DRAWING THE BIG RED MACHINE
Jerry Dowling
Published by Edgecliff Press, LLC., Cincinnati, Ohio
www.edgecliffpress.com

ISBN 9780984462223
Library of Congress Control Number 2010936797

10 9 8 7 6 5 4 3 2 1

Published in the United States of America

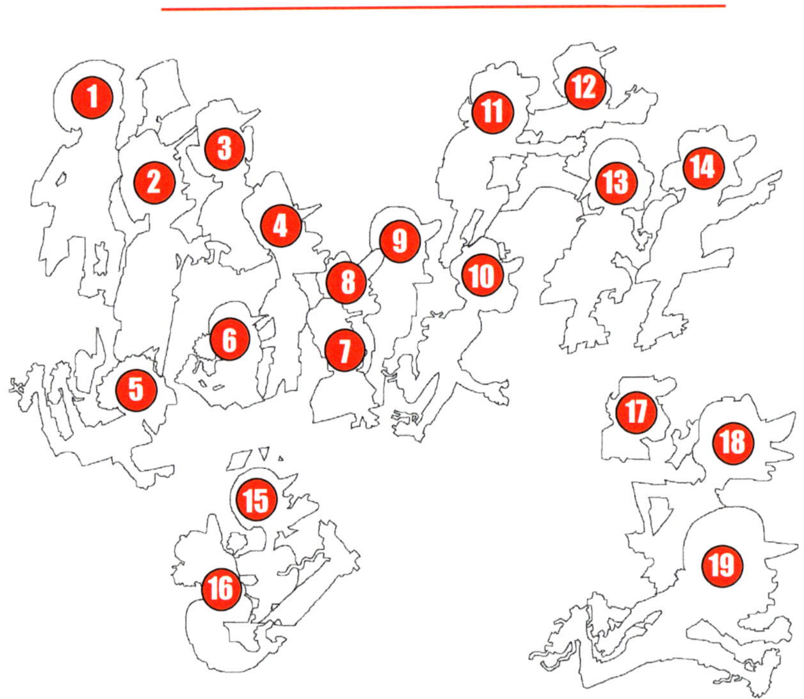

1. Marty Brennaman 2. Lou Piniella 3. Sparky Anderson 4. Eric Davis 5. Dave Concepcion 6. Tony Perez 7. Barry Larkin 8. Ken Griffey 9. Paul O'Neill 10. Gary Nolan 11. Tom Browning 12. Jose Rijo 13. Johnny Bench 14. Pete Rose 15. George Foster 16. Rob Dibble 17. Don Gullett 18. Chris Sabo 19. Joe Morgan

DEDICATED TO

GERALDINE

Hall of Fame wife

ACKNOWLEDGEMENTS and CREDITS

Sincere thanks go to all the people who assisted in one way or another with input, ideas, encouragement and advice. They are my family members and friends and associates (in no particular order), Ken Stewart, Terry Armor, Andy Furman, Walt Maher, Kit Andrews, Chris Payne, Mike Dodd, Mike Lopresti, Mark Schmetzer, former Cincinnati Enquirer Editors Jim Schottelkotte and Luke Feck, Zach Wells, Pat Barry and especially to Johnny Bench and Bob Quinn for penning the foreword and afterword.

PHOTO CREDITS

Ken Stewart, Gary Landers, Tad Barney, Ari Buchwald

SOURCES

Personal files, Google, Reds media guides.

IV Who is this guy?

This guy arrived in Cincinnati in late 1967 and immediately began drawing cartoons and illustrations for the *Cincinnati Enquirer*. After the introductory tasks of retouching photographs and laying out pages, he received one of his first assignments. The Art Director, 'little known' Ed Carr asked him to illustrate the 1968 Opening Day cover for the *Enquirer's* Special Section about the Reds. What better way to get noticed in the sports field!

The Reds were just beginning to develop the team which evolved into the powerhouse that ruled the baseball world for several years in the 70s. They had numerous colorful players which made it easy to draw their idiosyncrasies fairly regularly. Hence this big collection of Reds related art.

This guy also drew many entertainment and political people, including Elvis Presley and Frank Sinatra. While these were fun to portray, nothing could top drawing the Reds. He became a member of the Baseball Writers Association of America, and has a vote for the Hall of Fame in Cooperstown. Although retired, he still shows up in the press box at Great American Ball Park during most home games.

By the way, his name is Jerry Dowling.

HE LIES A LOT!

Foreword

By Johnny Bench, Hall of Fame catcher, Big Red Machine

Do you love sports and cartoons as much as I do? Well Jerry has given us his brilliant drawings in this book that will take us back to our favorite era when The Big Red Machine was dominating the 70s with power, speed, defense and pitching. I have always been a fan of Jerry and his sometimes zany way of seeing our lives on and off the field.

You will laugh out loud and take memory lane over and over again with this book.

Sparky was the driver of the Great Eight. Can you name them? Of course! Everyone knows Pete, Joe, Tony (The Big Dog) and me. Plus, you'll never forget Davey, George, Cesar and Ken. Can you name the starting pitchers? Jack, Gary, Don and Freddie. We can't forget our relievers, Zach and Will, Rawly, Pedro and Clay, The Hawk. It was a complete team and it took 25 players to win. Everyone contributed.

It was a close knit group of players that Bob Howsam put together. Back-to-back World Champions. Not too many teams can say that and millions of fans still believe that The Big Red Machine was the Greatest Team ever.

I do know that Jerry's book is the greatest. Get one for everybody. I will always be grateful that I can relive those days.

-Johnny Bench

This book is a collection of cartoons and illustrations about the years leading up to the Cincinnati Reds Big Red Machine baseball teams.

Although most fans regard the 1975 and 1976 squads as the REAL BRM, the Reds were being called that as far back as 1969.

The years following 1976 were usually contenders and the name stuck for a long time. Even the great 1990 team was sometimes considered part of that era.

The author of this book was an artist at *The Cincinnati Enquirer* and his writing experience was limited to injecting lines and comments into these original drawings. For this book, he wanted to describe and comment on each of the drawings. In producing this publication, he relied on memory and whatever research was available, so there will inevitably be a few mistakes. The author makes no claim to be a Pulitzer prize winner, so go easy on him and take these 'elaborations' in stride.

Some of these drawings are self contained, while others are part of a larger piece. Early on, the approach was to be rah-rah and very complimentary, but later, a tell-it-the-way-we-see-it way of thinking took over. Funny but fair.

Finally, the reproduction quality is as fine tuned as possible, considering that many were scanned from aging newsprint copies. The original art in some cases had deteriorated badly and couldn't copy very well. However, almost all of the color art is much better than it appeared in the newspaper, having been cleaned up for the book. Color registration in the old days was a hit and miss game, so enjoy what we have put together for you.

1969 Cranking up the machine

Cincinnati Enquirer - August 9, 1969

Cincinnati Enquirer - April 7, 1969

The well known version of the Big Red Machine which most fans identify with is the 1975-76 version. However, signs of dominance actually began in 1969 under the leadership of manager Dave Bristol and the first pictorial portrayal of that machine is shown above.

The Reds' power show became a regular event and a 19-run offensive destruction of the Philadelphia Phillies led to this drawing. The name itself had already been coined. Baseball writer Bob Hunter of the *Los Angeles Times* came up with the tag, although Pete Rose claims he was the originator, of course. There can be no dispute, however, that the author of this book drew the first visual depiction of the BRM.

The Reds themselves must have liked the image because they commissioned the artist to illustrate their 1969 Christmas card.

Cincinnati Reds - 1969

Cincinnati Enquirer - July 14, 1969

The Big Bopper — first baseman Lee May was the team's Bopperest.

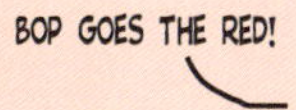

1970

The Sparky plug!

Cincinnati Enquirer - 1970

George Lee "Sparky" Anderson was hired by general manager Bob Howsam to take over from Dave Bristol as manager of the Machine. He was only 35.

Anderson played one season in the majors as a second baseman for the Philadelphia Phillies, batting a lowly .218.

This author had heard of Sparky, having seen him play for the minor league Toronto Maple Leafs when he lived there in the early 60s. Sparky became manager of that team in 1964, ending his playing career.

It didn't take long for the 1970 squad to let their division foes know who was going to be the force by winning 70 of the first 100 games. They built a huge lead, playing in Crosley Field until June 30, when the new Riverfront Stadium was ready. Tony Perez led the attack and with Johnny Bench and Lee May. They simply had too much power. Even bit players such as outfielder Ty Cline and relief specialist Wayne Granger were vital clogs in the Machine.

BITTY BITTY BANG BANG!

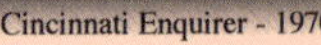

Cincinnati Enquirer - 1970

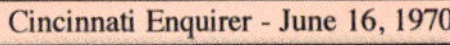

Cincinnati Enquirer - June 16, 1970

The '70 model has a few changes!

Cincinnati Enquirer - May 8, 1970

As The Song Says . . . 'It's One, Two, Three And He's Out Of The Old Ball Game!'

Cincinnati Enquirer - June 12, 1970

Down by the water

On June 30, 1970, the Reds said so long to dilapidated Crosley Field and hauled their equipment (players included) to the brand new multi-purpose stadium on the shores of the beautiful stench pond, the Ohio River. Some of the scenery was feces pieces of Pittsburgh floating by. The stadium deal involved sharing the building with an expansion professional football team, the Bengals.

Rookie pitcher Wayne Simpson typified the Reds' hot start of the 1970 season, by dousing opposition hitters. He racked up a 14-3 record. His season ended early with a bad arm, and he wasn't the same after. He was traded later to Kansas City for Roger Nelson, a big pitcher with large shoulder blades — nothing else. Oh, and noted Richie Scheinblum.

Future Hall of Famer Johnny Bench had a huge year, smashing 45 homers and 148 RBIs.

Cincinnati Enquirer - June 30, 1970

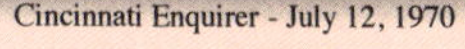
Cincinnati Enquirer - July 12, 1970

Cincinnati Enquirer - June 26, 1970

Cincinnati Enquirer - July 31, 1970

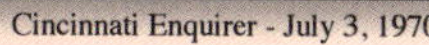
Cincinnati Enquirer - July 3, 1970

Pair of wet dirty rats!

Hiding in my ink bottle for a couple years was this little rodent, Dirty Rat. He finally flipped his lid and popped out of his hole. He had arms, which I later amputated and he became just a head case.

MY COMMENTS ARE ALL WET!

Bubbly celebration!

Cincinnati Enquirer - September, 1970

A nice cool libation was in order after the great season the Reds put together.

Even though it seemed as if the tank was emptying late in the year, there were still a few drops left to keep the machine running.

The Reds clinched the National League Western Division title early enough that they could watch the battle in the East to see who would be the next foe on the way to the league pennant.

It might be the Pirates, Mets, or the Cubs.

Cincinnati Enquirer - September, 1970

Let The Shoot-Out Begin

The sun in Pittsburgh will be high in the sky and the streets barren of people. It is the day of the shoot-out . . . the day when the best in the West — the Cincinnati Reds — and that cool dude from the East — the Pittsburgh Pirates — square off head-to-head and face-to-face.

As in a Western shoot-out, this is a do-or-die affair. For the loser there is no tomorrow, nothing left to say but "Wait 'Til Next Year." For the winner there is even a bigger gun fight around the corner, a battle with the champion of the American League in the World Series.

This is no ordinary gunfight that begins at 1 p.m. today at Three Rivers Stadium, Pittsburgh. Sis-shooters aren't the weapons. Instead, it will bas in the National League go against one another.

The artillery will be supplied for Cincinnati by Johnny Bench, Tony Perez and Lee May, three men who hit more the 30 homers each during the National League season. The Pirates counter with the likes of Roberto Clemente, a mere .355 hitter; power-packed Willie Stargell and young Bob Robertson.

Both sides have [illegible] firepower — Pete Rose, Bobby Tolan and Bernie Carbo for Cincinnati, Richie Hebner, Manny Sanguillen, Gene Alley, Mattie Alou and BillMazeroski for Pittsburgh, and remember that Mazeroski killed off some damned Yankees in an earlier year with a cannon shot long remembered.

Yes, the victory doesn't figure to go to the fastest gun in this one, just the one that lets out with the bigger boom.

This is a shoot-out, 1970-style, and most of all, National League style. So let it all begin.

Cincinnati Enquirer - October 3, 1970

Cincinnati Enquirer - October, 1970

Eleventh hour battles

The Pittsburgh Pirates emerged as the winners of the National League Eastern division, outdistancing the Chicago Cubs and New York Mets by 5 and 6 games respectively.

The Reds then handily completed a three game sweep of the Bucs (who also had a brand new riverfront ballyard) to capture the National League title for the first time since 1961.

Then it was on it to the World Series to take on a flock of Baltimore birds.

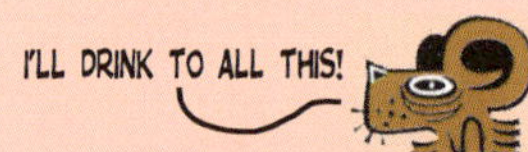

For the record

Fleetwood Records, 1970

As explained in the first book of this series, "DRAWING PETE!", I was commissioned by Fleetwood Records to illustrate this record album cover. Being available nationwide, the album title solidified the name BIG RED MACHINE, and it pretty much established this artist as the visual portrayer of the vehicle.

It was a collection of actual 1970 Reds game broadcasts, narrated by Jim McIntyre and the legendary Joe Nuxhall. Joe's initial radio stint began in 1967 with McIntyre until the arrivals of Al Michaels in 1971 and Marty Brennaman three years later. Joe and Marty were a team through the 2007 season, ending only with Joe's passing that fall.

It was Al Michaels' first season calling Reds and he was so astonished by the team's incredible power, that he exclaimed "So this is The Big Red Machine! I like it!"

DON'T BREAK THIS RECORD!

1971 Sparky's gang

Cincinnati Enquirer - April 5, 1971

Having lost the 1970 World Series to Brooks Robinson and the Baltimore Orioles, the Reds were hoping the 1971 season would turn out better. Players surrounding Sparky are, clockwise from the top left, Johnny Bench, Hal McRae, Tony Perez, Lee May, Dave Concepcion, Bernie Carbo, Pete Rose and Tommy Helms.

High hopes, low results

After such a fine 1970 season, the Reds figured to be the team to beat this year. Not so, with the exception of young Don Gullett, who fired up a 16-6 won and loss mark, their performance was quality challenged.

Even future Hall of Famer catcher Johnny Bench saw his power stats drop significantly, going from 45 homers in 1970 to only 27 long balls. He drove in 87 **LESS** runs than the previous year. It was Pirates slugger Willie Stargell who put on the power show, belting 48 home runs.

Reds-Letter -November, 1971

Al Michaels teamed with a young lefthander Joe Nuxhall to call Reds games in 1971.

Cincinnati Enquirer - April 5, 1971

Cincinnati Enquirer - 1971

Klunkers!

Fortunately, the Reds version of the ill-fated Edsel vehicle lasted only one year, while the Ford Motor Company tried theirs for three dismal years before cutting it loose.

Pitcher Jim McGlothlin was part of the 1971 rotation, but was one of the weaker parts of the Machine, going only 8-12.

Cincinnati Enquirer - 1971

Cincinnati Enquirer - December 10, 1971

Cincinnati Enquirer - 1971

ALMOST FORGOTTEN HISTORY!

1972
BIG JOHN!

Not the same BIG BAD JOHN as singer Jimmy Dean's guy, but ten years later, the Reds' BAD BOY might have been even 'BADDER' — at least to National League hurlers.

Big Bad Johnny Bench administered another beating to the National League opposition in 1972. By smacking them with his hands and bat, Johnny was the West Division champ.

Cincinnati Enquirer - April 2, 1972

A BIGGER, BADDER HIT PARADE!

The real dealer!

Failing in his attempt to deal in a major league baseball franchise in Denver, master gambler Bob Howsam's next bluff was to start a rival league, the Continental. After that hand folded, he next played some St. Louis 'Cards'. Joining that squad in mid-season 1964, he led it to a World Series title, downing the New York Yankees. Howsam later drew a couple aces, Orlando Cepeda and Roger Maris, who played winning 'Card' hands in 1967-68.

Bob debarked the 1967 St. Louis cruise early, and paddled his way up river to the port of Cincinnati, where he became the Real Riverfront Gambler.

Trader Bob played the right cards in 1972, discarding popular Lee May and Tommy Helms while picking up aces Joe Morgan, Cesar Geronimo and Jack Billingham from the Houston Astros.

Morgan immediately became a base specialist, swiping 58 of them while playing a Gold Glove second base. His partner in crime, Bobby Tolan, added 42 stolen sacks.

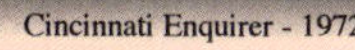

Cincinnati Enquirer - 1972

Cincinnati Enquirer - 1972

Collectors item

The Reds had scheduled several promotion days, but none had the importance of the last one, winning the pennant for the fans.

Cincinnati Enquirer - September 15, 1972

The thinker!

Creative Cincinnati sculptor Sparky "Rodin" Anderson chopped off huge chunks of opposition rocks until he was satisfied with his masterpiece, "DIVISION TITLE".

Reds-Letter - August, 1972

COMMAND PILOT BENCH!

Cincinnati Enquirer - 1972

Almost home!

Maybe it was that Astronaut connection that put the Big Reds Rocket into an 11-1 victory orbit around the National League.

Left in the tracks

The Los Angeles Dodgers and the Houston Astros were flattened by ten and a half games each by the Big Red Machine in the West. The rest of that division's teams didn't even get that close.

How The West Was Won

By BOB HERTZEL
Enquirer Sports Reporter

HOUSTON—It started with a shock, this rush to the Western Division championship of the National League, and ended right here in Texas with the Cincinnati Reds rolling over their No. 1 adversary, the Houston Astros.

The road was bumpy at the start, filled with rocks and pot-holes. But, once the Big Red Machine made the right turn, it was all expressway to the title. This is how it went:

NOVEMBER 29—Hands shaking, voice cracking, Reds' public relations director Roger Ruhl announces in Phoenix, Ariz., that Cincinnati has traded All-Star first baseman Lee May, second baseman Tommy Helms and utility player Jimmy Stewart to Houston for second baseman Joe Morgan, third baseman Denis Menke, pitcher Jack Billingham and outfielders Cesar Geronimo and Ed Armbrister. The deal draws heavy criticism but starts the Reds toward the title. General Manager Bob Howsam still hasn't made a blunder.

DECEMBER 6—The Reds, not knowing if Bobby Tolan will be able to play due to ruptured achilles tenden that kept him out of action for all of 1971, trade young pitcher Milt Wilcox to Cleveland for Ted Uhlaender.

DECEMBER 3—Howsam does it again. Reliever Wayne Granger goes to Minnesota for left-hander Tom Hall.

FEBRUARY 25—Reds open spring training. Bobby Tolan vows he'll be in Opening Day lineup. Sparky Anderson predicts a tight race in West with his team in it all the way. Tolan's right; Anderson's wrong. The race isn't tight.

APRIL 1—The Reds are ready to open the season. Marvin Miller and the owners aren't and strike hits baseball.

APRIL 6—Traditional Opening Day in Cincinnati is cancelled as players remain on strike. Reds work out at University of Cincinnati

APRIL 15—Opening Day comes at last. Strike is over and the Reds begin their pennant chase. What a beginning, bowing 3-1 to Dodgers before 37,895 in Riverfront Stadium. Nervous Morgan has auspicious debut with 0-for-3 and an error. Tolan keeps vow and is in lineup, fans three times. Denis Menke hits first Reds' homer of year.

APRIL 16—The Runnin' Reds are born as Reds win first game behind Gary Nolan, 10-1, over Dodgers. Morgan and Tolan each steal two bases, Dave Concepcion steals one.

APRIL 18—The day of decision . . . Reds vs. Astros for first time in 1972. Astros win, 8-4, despite Tolan's 4 for 4.

APRIL 19—Astros beat Reds and Billingham, 7-5, and the season is off to a horrible start.

APRIL 25—Things still going lousy for Reds as Pirates' Richie Hebner hits three-run homer in 13th to give Bucs a 5-2 victory despite Johnny Bench's first homer of the season.

MAY 1—This is sick. Cardinals rock Don Gullett early, take 6-0 lead. Reds come back and win, 7-6, but send Gullett home to hospital where it's learned he has hepatitis.

MAY 5—Bench's hit in 10th beats Pirates, 5-4, lifting Reds' record to 8-9. Wayne Simpson and Ross Grimsley are recalled from Indianapolis.

MAY 10—Rock bottom. Reds drop fourth in a row, fall to 8-13. Will Sparky make it to the All-Star break? How could Howsam have made such a trade?

MAY 11—Grimsley makes first start, beats St. Louis, 5-4.

MAY 13—Simpson makes first start, beats St. Louis, 11-2. The Reds are rolling.

MAY 14—Reds sweep doubleheader from Cards to make it four in a row, Perez winning first game with homer and driving in both runs of 2-0 victory in the second game. Tom Hall comes out of the bullpen to hurl Reds' first complete game and shutout of year, fanning 12.

MAY 12—It had to happen. Nine-game winning streak ends as San Diego and Steve Arlin beat Reds, 5-1.

MAY 29—This is it. Four games out and on to Houston for four-game series. Reds establish superiority. Win opener, 8-3, drawing 10 walks with newcomer Joe Hague driving in four runs.

MAY 30—Johnny Bench takes over with two homers, a single and four runs batted in as Reds beat Astros, 9-5.

MAY 31—It's Bench again with single, double and homer, three runs batted in as Reds whip Astros, 12-4. Oh, yes. George Foster hits a grand slam homer.

JUNE 1—Johnny Bench completes sweep of Houston with homer, single and two walks while Hal McRae hits a pinch hit grand slam homer. Reds win, 10-3.

JUNE 3—Things are coming up roses. Losing 5-0 to Steve Carlton and Phillies, Reds come back and win, 6-5.

JUNE 25—After long, hard struggle for the lead, Reds take over first place for good in the West with a 4 victory over, of all people, Houston. And the winning run? Driven in by Menke with a double in 10th inning.

JULY 2—Nate Colbert of Padres hits homer off Clay Carroll, ending the right-hander's unbelievable streak of 20 consecutive appearances without allowing a run.

JULY 11—Billingham shuts out Pittsburgh, 5-0, and a seven-game winning streak begins.

JULY 13—Gary Nolan wins [illegible] in a row to run his record to 13 [illegible]

JULY 19—Nolan sent home from Chicago with arm trouble. Misses the All-Star game.

AUGUST 4—Nolan comes back, has more arm trouble.

AUGUST 12—Reds drop third in a row, Houston is sneaking up.

AUGUST 13—Reds start nine of 10 win streak.

AUGUST 28—Nolan returns, gives up just one hit over six innings. He's cured.

SEPTEMBER 1—Pete Rose breaks Vada Pinson's all-time club record for hits with 1882nd of career.

SEPTEMBER 11 — Bench drives in his 100th run of the year as Reds whip Giants, 8-7.

SEPTEMBER 22—There's no magic number. Reds win.

WORLD SERIES
WEST
REDS
ANDERSON
'72 SEASON

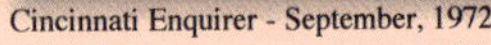
Cincinnati Enquirer - September, 1972

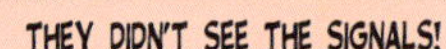
THEY DIDN'T SEE THE SIGNALS!

What jinx?

Maybe the Big Red Machine experienced a vehicular sophomore jinx in 1971. Regardless, the boys certainly had something to prove to the foe. They did so by pulling away to a Western Division title by a whopping ten and a half game win over the Los Angeles Dodgers and the Houston Astros.

'Lee'ding men!

Captain Hook, as George Lee "Sparky" Anderson was tagged because of his penchant for yanking pitchers before further damage occurred, was named his league's manager of the year four times, the first of which was the 1972 season. This was to be the second division title in his first three years at the Machine helm.

And the other Lee, Johnny Lee Bench, was back in power form, showing that 1971 was actually an off season, by belting 40 round trippers and driving in 125.

Bench also struck fear in opposing pitchers to the tune of 100 walks. Fast for a catcher, he stole quite a few bases as well.

Cincinnati Enquirer - 1972

Cincinnati Enquirer - 1972

Cincinnati Enquirer - October 11, 1972

Surprises, surprises!

In game four of the 1972 NL championship series against the Pittsburgh Pirates, the Reds won 7-1. Speedy catcher Bench stole two bases. Winning hurler Ross Grimsley gave up only two hits, as many as he clubbed himself.

Battery batterers!

It seems that using the image of The Big Red Machine gives this artist a huge fund of cartoon ideas. This one is no exception, as the Pirates vandalized the tank by clobbering the Reds in Game 3 at Three Rivers Stadium in Pittsburgh.

With the pitching arm of closer Dave Giusti and the bat of catcher Manny Sanguillen, they had reduced the Machine to a pile of scrap metal. The Reds squeaked by in Game 5, beating relief ace Giusti with two runs in the 9th inning.

Cincinnati Enquirer - October, 1972

Western weirdos

Cincinnati Enquirer - October 14, 1972

Eccentric isn't a good enough adjective to describe the wackiness of Oakland A's owner Charlie Finley.

Charlie started the goofiness in Kansas City before he moved his team to Oakland, using orange baseballs, having a rabbit doll pop out of the ground to hand balls to the umpire, dressing his pet mule Charlie O. in a team uniform, giving pitcher Satchel Paige a lounge chair in the bullpen — the list is endless.

He dressed his entire team in bright yellow and Kelly green uniforms, with white shoes.

He ordered his players to grow beards, mustaches and long hair. Some say he banned deodorant.

Anyway, this is what the Reds faced in the 1972 World Series.

Fill 'er up!

After running on fumes the last few games of the division playoffs, the dented and smashed Big Red Machine needed refueling for the trip west to take on Charlie Finley's West Coast Wackos, erstwhile known as the Oakland A's.

Three days after the bruising Pirate series, the Reds arrived in Oakland ready to apply that black and blue color combo to Finley's crayon clad clods.

Cincinnati Enquirer - October, 1972

1973 Out of the dark

Cincinnati Enquirer - 1973

Things looked bright with young Gary Nolan coming off a great 15-5 won-loss record in 1972. With Kansas City ace Roger Nelson arriving royally from Kansas City by trade, things looked very sunny.

Well, the dimmer switch soon came on as Nolan, battling arm and shoulder injuries throughout his career, didn't win a single game. Nelson was anything but lights out to the opposition, winning only three. He got lit up regularly.

One bulb that was on constantly was the hat-eating (more about that later) Pedro Borbon. He was acquired in the deal that got defensive dimbulb Alex Johnson unscrewed in 1969.

Speaking of screws, Pedro seemed to be missing a few himself, but who cared when he shut off the opposing lights.

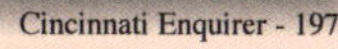
Cincinnati Enquirer - 1973

Cincinnati Enquirer - April 13, 1973

Reds checkered flag

Another important cog of the Machine from the Astros deal was lanky Jack Billingham, who put together a 19-10 record in 1973, making sure that the tank never went dry.

It looked like the Riverfront gas attendant siphoned the needed fuel from the Los Angeles Dodgers. By saving the pit stops, the Big Red Machine pulled away late in the race to capture the National League West flag.

Cincinnati Enquirer - 1973

Cincinnati Enquirer - 1973

Mets Win East Title: Meet Reds In Playoff

CHICAGO (AP) — The New York Mets, in last place as recently as August 31, clinched the National League's East Division title Monday — one day after the scheduled close of the regular baseball season — with a 6-4 victory over the Chicago Cubs.

The Mets will now face the West Division winners, the Cincinnati Reds, in a best-of-five playoff for the National League title. That series begins Saturday in Cincinnati.

The winner will advance to the World Series, which begins October 13, against the winner of the American League playoff between the Oakland A's and Baltimore Orioles, which also starts Saturday.

The St. Louis Cardinals finished in second place in the National League East with an 81-81 record. Pittsburgh finished at 80-82 after losing to the Padres 4-3. (See details in the Sports Section.)

Cincinnati Enquirer - October 2, 1973

Never gets old!

The Big Red Machine as most fans identify with was really taking shape in 1973. Joe Morgan was firmly installed at second base, Cesar Geronimo took over in center field and Ken Griffey arrived to play right field. Dave Concepcion was pushing Darrel Chaney out of the shortstop spot. George 'Yahtzee' Foster had been acquired from the San Francisco Giants in 1971 for rusty parts Frank Duffy and Vern Geishert. All the parts fit!

In the National League championship battles, the main event featured Pete Rose vs. New York Mets shortstop Bud Harrelson. On the undercard, Pedro 'the Dominican Dracula', Borbon took a bite out of the hat of Mets hurler Buzz Capra. The Mets, however, proved to be hungrier than the Big Red Machine, devouring the Reds 3 games to two.

Cincinnati Enquirer - 1974

Cincinnati Enquirer - 1974

Cincinnati Enquirer - July 10, 1974

1974

Taking a break

Unlike 1971, the Reds had a very good record, only to fall 4 games short of the Los Angeles Dodgers. They pushed the westerners to the end, causing Ron 'the penguin' Cey to hear big footsteps.

Not even noted race car mechanic George Bignotti could repair the damage caused by a late western trip

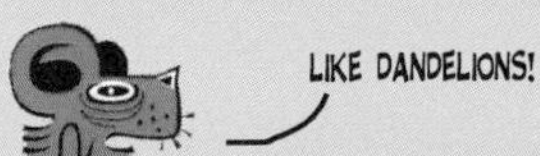

1975

Speedball!

Cincinnati Enquirer - January 26, 1975

Artificial grass, such as the AstroTurf installed at Riverfront Stadium, allowed ground balls to speed through the infield much quicker than on natural turf.

Slugger George Foster liked having his batting average go higher because of that, while pitcher Fred Norman figured it would also raise his earned run average.

Cincinnati Enquirer - June, 1975

Slugging and chugging!

This time, the Big Red Machine took to the rails, chugging its way to the top of the division and about to glide down to a successful end.

Stoking the fire were the offensive shovellers Johnny Bench, Tony Perez, Joe Morgan and Pete Rose. Steering the engine was the engineer Gary Nolan and his assistant Don Gullett, combining for 30 wins against a mere 13 defeats.

Cincinnati Enquirer - July, 1975

Early and out!

Any thoughts of the Dodgers had of catching the Big Red Machine were put out of their minds by the Reds late inning comeback victories. The Bums waved the white flag of concession early, finishing twenty games behind the Reds 108 win season.

Just to put a lid on the season, and to leave no doubt as to which team was the best in the division, the local boys won eleven of the final twelve games.

Cincinnati Enquirer - July, 1975

Reds-Letter - January, 1975

Gloves of Gold!

The 1975 Big Red Machine could just as well been tagged the Big Gold Glove Machine, as they built up a collection of those glittering gloves as impressive as the Queen's royal jewels.

The Reds middle defense had more gold than Fort Knox. That defense was so tight that very few offensive assaults got past it.

The infield moat monsters were Johnny Bench at the drawbridge, with Joe Morgan and Dave Concepcion guarding the infield gate.

If by chance, anything got past that security, there was center fielder Cesar Geronimo to gobble up the leftovers.

Tiempo de comida (chow time)

There's always an ample supply of food in the Reds clubhouse but Pedro Borbon needed more fiber added to his dietary requirements. Baseball hats were his meals of choice, starting with the Mets' Buzz Capra's in the 1973 NL division playoffs, and now the cap of teammate Cesar Geronimo.

Later in his career, Pedro added a few appetizers. He found Pirate pitcher Daryl Patterson's ear to be savory, and for a midnight snack he ate a disco bouncer's cheek. For steak he loved the taste and texture of rented furniture.

Cincinnati Enquirer -August 1, 1975

Author's note: I admit to knowing absolutely no Spanish. The words herein are courtesy of a fellow Enquirer artist so any grammatical or wording errors must be blamed on George "Peruvian Dudie" Longfellow.

Complete what they start!

Pat Darcy, was best known for serving up the famous home run to Boston Red Sox catcher Carlton Fisk in the 12th inning of game 6 of the 1975 World Series. He had one good season out of the three he was with the Big Red Machine, going 11-5. Pat kept Sparky's hook sharpened, being at the end of it 21 times in 22 starts. This cartoon depicts his 'career' start — his one and only complete game. It was a surprise to everybody.

Injury plagued southpaw Don Gullett had the same number of starts as Darcy, but completed eight of them. Few pitchers today come close to that total. Don's won-loss mark was 15-4 in 1975. By comparison, Jack Billingham and Gary Nolan each started 32 games and finished only four, while lefty Fred Norman only completed two of 34 starts. Other starter Clay Kirby was one for 19. Sparky wore out his hook on those four.

Joe Morgan completed games in different ways by stealing them. He walked a career high 132 times and stole 67 bases. That's like 199 doubles. Joe also had 27 two baggers that season so there he was at second 226 times. Pretty amazing! While Morgan was scoring 107 runs, he also found time to drive in 94. A Little Red Run Machine!

Cincinnati Enquirer - August, 1975

DON'T GET ME STARTED!

Cincinnati Enquirer - September, 1975

Cincinnati Enquirer - August, 1975

Go figure!

Cincinnati Enquirer - September, 1975

Switching roles, even temporarily, were Darrel Chaney and catcher Johnny Bench. Darrel wasn't even the regular shortstop, as Davey Concepcion was firmly ensconced at that position. He managed a grand total of two home runs, while Bench led the team with 28 long ones, but stole eleven bases, a great total for a backstop.

Cincinnati Enquirer - September, 1975

Please!

For various reasons, Sparky didn't give the playoff first game ball to any of the three pitchers here. It slipped through all their hands and landed in the paws of lefty Don Gullett.

Billingham hadn't appeared a whole lot in the final days, while Clay Kirby was the odd man left out.

Picking Gullett was a wise selection, for the farmboy from Kentucky not only tossed a complete game win, 8-3, but homered and drove in three runs.

Rather than wasting this space on Danny Murtaugh's chin, we'll use it to show Sparky explaining the odds of winning the playoffs to him.

Cincinnati Enquirer - October 4, 1975

Pirating the Bucs!

The Big Red Machine put on the power/speed show which led it to 108 wins during the season. It simply continued in the National League playoffs against the Pittsburgh Pirates as the Reds swept the foe in three straight.

Outscoring the Pirates in the series 19-7, the Cincinnati marauders sank the enemy with a bunch of cannonball hits and base plundering.

Meanwhile, over in the A.L., the Bostonians were doing the same, whipping Charlie Finley's Oakland team of bearded beasts, 3-0.

Cincinnati Enquirer - October, 1975

KICKED THEIR MULES!

Cheers to Pete!

Pete Rose agreed (or likely was told by Sparky) to move to third base. This opened the left field spot for power-hitting George Foster, and allowed Tony Perez to shift across the diamond to first base.

Making tracks

To celebrate the successful end of the 1975 National League season, this cartoon showed the Big Red Machine laying tracks on the way to Boston. The latest tread made its mark, following the 1970 and 1972 prints.

We wizards at *The Enquirer* used this drawing as a basis the special graphic (below right). Special ink was used so the readers could cut the drawing from the newspaper and iron it into t-shirts. No, we aren't using that ink in this book.

Cincinnati Enquirer - October, 1975

Cincinnati Enquirer - October 8, 1975

Cincinnati Enquirer - October, 1975

Cincinnati Enquirer - October, 1975

Seriesously...

This cartoon series, Pen-Pourri, ran once or twice week in *The Enquirer* for several years. It was always a group of similar themes depicting current sports events.

This one made fun of a few 1975 World Series occurrences.

Johnny Bench got his bat going — Pete was known for the way he dived into bases and the Red Sox outfielders dived after balls.

Boston third base coach Don "The Gerbil" Zimmer seemed to have a penchant for sending his runners to their doom at home plate.

Cincinnati Enquirer -October 11, 1975

What's up Jack? The pot?

The Big Boys of the Red Machine were already hauling in big bucks, by 1975 standards, and they stood to rake in a bigger pile by winning the World Series.

It was flabbergasting to think that one baseball player would command a salary above $100,000 per season, let alone four of them — on the same team!

It was led by Pete Rose, who in 1970 had claimed he wanted to be the first singles hitter to make a hundred grand. He did, signing for $105,000. (Note: In 2005, Pete's hit record bat sold for over $100,000 alone, cork and all). In 1975, Pete was paid $165,000, and he pulled teammates salaries up also. Johnny Bench hauled in $150,000, Joe Morgan made $132,500 and Tony Perez collected $100,000.

But this just proves the old saying that you get what you pay for.

Since then, the pot has been jacked up big time, with even the Major League minimum salary in 2010 being $400,000 per season, plus per diem.

I'LL TAKE A SPLIT!

Big Red Sea attack!

Spying on the home of the Boston Red Sox, the Big Red Machine's 1975 World Series opponent, were Captain Hook Sparky Anderson and his first mate starter Don Gullett.

The two had one specific purpose of this sneak attack — to destroy Boston pitcher Luis Tiant.

Something went wrong however, as Tiant and the Sox sank the Big Red Ship into the Charles River by the score of 6-0, to take a one game lead.

Cincinnati Enquirer -October 11, 1975

The 1975 World Series!

Cincinnati Enquirer October, 1975

Boston Red Sox catcher Carlton Fisk was involved in one of the most controversial World Series calls ever. It was made by home plate umpire Larry Barnett who, according to Fisk, failed to call interference on Reds Ed Armbrister, resulting in a Fisk throwing error which led to the Reds winning run in Game 3. Fisk later slammed the famous 12th inning home run which won Game 6 for the Sox.

Big Red Sox Weight Machine Reggie Cleveland, imitated a huge blimp which the Reds deflated in Game 5. The winning hurler in that game was Reds ace Don Gullett.

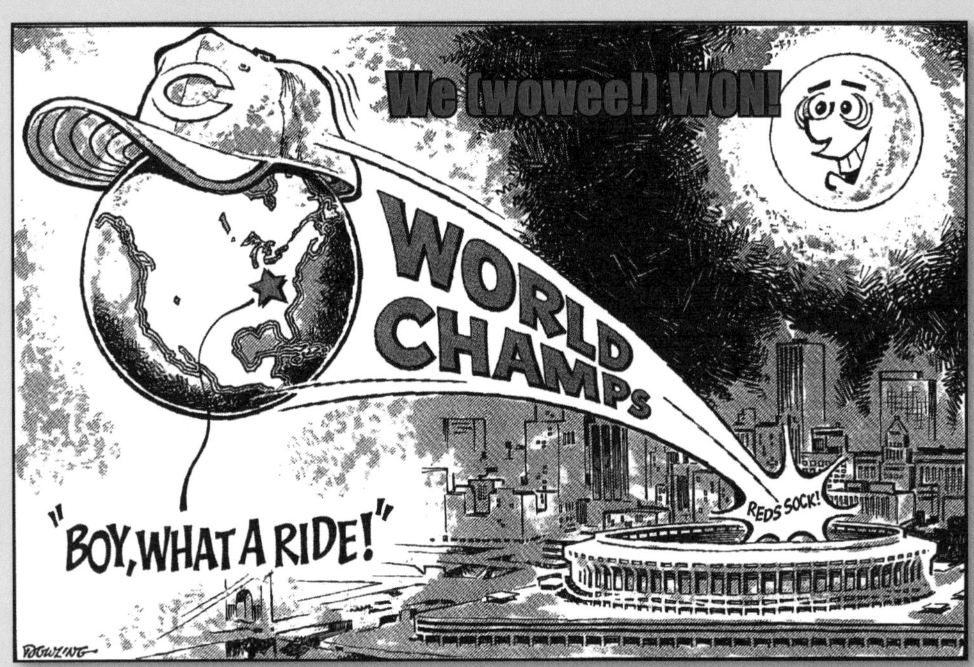

Cincinnati Enquirer - October, 1975

Borrowing the famous Ohioan John Glenn's line seemed to fit the way the Big Red Machine orbited the baseball world. This journey required seven trips around the globe before finally landing in Boston's Fenway Park. The intended touchdown site Riverfront Stadium had to wait until the team arrived home the next day. A huge celebration then was held at Fountain Square in downtown Cincinnati.

We (sob!) LOST!

What could be more pitiful than NBC's Curt Gowdy announcing the 1975 World Series where his beloved Red Sox dropped the final game and the poor guy had to call the last catch. A sadder look has never been seen.

Hurt Curt

Cincinnati Enquirer - October, 1975

Cincinnati Enquirer - October, 1975

And the winner is...

The Reds were World Champions. None of Cincinnati's other sports franchises came close to winning their leagues. Tony Mason's UC Bearcats were only 6-5. Paul Brown's Bengals lost in the playoffs, while Terry Slater's pucksters missed the playoffs.

Future Reds ace Tom Seaver won his third Cy Young award, but he was a couple years from being a Big Red Machine member.

Cincinnati Enquirer - November, 1975

How's about Howsam?

Winning the championship in 1975 wasn't enough to satisfy Trader Bob Howsam.

He kept the phone busy, wheeling and dealing, and ordering airplane tickets for various players' flights in and out of town.

At the departure gate was questionable stalwart infielder Darrel Chaney. More surprising players sent out of the exit door were pitchers Clay Kirby, Joaquin Andujar and fan favorite Clay "Hawk" Carroll.

Landing in Greater Cincinnati were outfielders Bob Bailey and Mike Lum, along with pitcher Jeff Sovern.

Cincinnati Enquirer - December 16, 1975

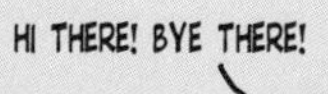

Big Red Machine book #1

Bob Hertzel
THE BIG RED MACHINE®
The Inside Story of Baseball's Best Team

Prentice-Hall - 1976

The book you are reading right now is just one of the several gazillion books that have been published about the Big Red Machine. The one on this page is undoubtably the very first one, penned by *The Cincinnati Enquirer's* Reds beat writer Bob Hertzel in 1976. Bob asked this artist to illustrate the cover.

Bob covered the Reds for several years, outlasting almost all the others with the possible exception of the current *Enquirer* writer John Fay, and the Hall of Famer Hal McCoy of *The Dayton Daily News*, who, although retired after 37 years on the beat, is still active as a freelancer and is a regular in the press box.

The writer of this book didn't actually 'cover' the Reds, but was in the press box way back to the days of Crosley Field, taking notes and making sketches for future cartoon reference. He can still be found in the Great American Ball Park press box during most home games.

This book may be one of many on the BRM, but it is unique in that it's the only one full of cartoons and illustrations of the team.

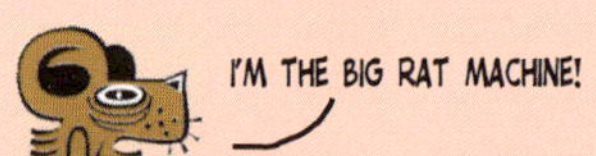

Got everything!

With 108 regular season wins, a playoff victory topped with the 1975 World Series title, what else could Sparky ask Santa for at Christmas except more of the same?

Captain Hook might have asked for some better pitching, the weak spot on the team, or maybe a new hook for removing the hurlers from the mound. Hair dye was a possibility, although Sparky stopped using it a year or so before.

Maybe a spell check for his typewriter. (What's a typewriter?)

Cincinnati Enquirer - December 23, 1975

1976

Sparky's pluggers!

This cartoon was drawn to go accompany a story about some lady complaining about players openly chewing tobacco in the dugout and on the field. It looks as if she was about to shoot a photo for evidence.

Noted Big Red chewers included the boss Sparky, coach Alex Grammas, infielder Darrel Chaney and bench warmer Merv Rettenmund. Even catcher Johnny Bench was a chewer. We don't know how often he had to call time to wipe his mask clean. Rettenmund was a seldom used outfielder whose couple decent seasons were in the past, brought in by Trader Bob, mainly to pinch hit. He was very creative with preparing his chaw, marinating it in a soda and then wrapping it inside chewed bubble gum.

Cincinnati Enquirer - April 1, 1976

Cagey guys!

In Atlanta's Fulton County Stadium bullpen (Riverfront had no bullpen as the relief corps sat in the dugout until needed), Pitching coach Larry Shepard wandered out to get somebody up and ready. He opened the bullpen door only to discover that his relievers were warming up with a different kind of ball...the basket type. The Braves groundskeepers had erected a makeshift court, and it might be assumed that a similar one was made for the former Braves reliever Gene Conley, a 6'8" guy, who also played in the National Basketball Association.

Cincinnati Enquirer - April 2, 1976

Ruling the world

Cincinnati Reds - 1976

Sparky was resting easy on top of the world, having led the Machinery to the World Championship in 1975, defeating the Boston Red Sox in seven terrific games. To make sure he stayed up there were supporting stars of the baseball galaxy Tony Perez, Pete Rose, Joe Morgan and Johnny Bench. There were also many other stellar satellites orbiting this huge planet.

MARS? THIS IS THE REAL RED PLANET!

Cincinnati Enquirer - April 9, 1976

Confidence!

Frequently the sports sections left little layout holes. Dirty Rat became a filler for a while, producing small cartoons to fit. Sparky's comments here weren't strong enough for a major drawing, so here he is with a simple prediction. After winning 108 game in 1975, he was very cautious in predicting only 90 wins this year.

With the same powerful engine running the Big Red Machine in 1976, there wasn't much tune up needed to begin the new race.

Cincinnati Enquirer - April 8, 1976

Cincinnati Enquirer - April 9, 1976

Buzz off!

The brand new Cincinnati Stingers hockey team had just finished their initial season in the World Hockey Association, next door in the Coliseum, and wound up in last place. Still upset at the way their season ended, they attacked the Reds ballpark next door.

Bob Howsam's assistant, Dick Wagner first tried to use a fire extinguisher to disperse the bees who were attacking everything behind home plate, including television equipment and microphones.

Finally, some professional beekeepers in attendance got the job done.

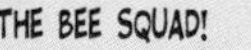

The other bench

When you think of the Big Red Machine bench, it's almost automatic Johnny that pops up in your mind.

The other bench, aka the extra guys riding the pine were either available as pinch hitters or runners late in the game. Or as it was occurring too often early in the season, they were stranded out on the bases.

Cincinnati Enquirer - May 14, 1976

Cincinnati Enquirer - May 4, 1976

Cincinnati Enquirer - May 16, 1976

Kids bats and gloves

Little fans, future stars! The Kid Glove game kids love the Big Red Machine and idols like Jack Billingham and George Foster.

Cincinnati Enquirer -May 25, 1976

Drawing shorts

Because Pen-Pourri was a regular feature in the sports pages of *The Enquirer* during the great years of the Big Red Machine, the artist was luckily able to portray many individuals of those teams. Here are three of which Santo Alcala was part. He probably wouldn't have had any of himself alone. He had a spectacular, albeit extremely short tenure with the Reds. He won 11 games in 1976, then only three more as his major league career ended after two years. Captain Hook removed him regularly, because he completed only three games out of 32 starts and his earned run average was a horrible 4.70.

Pen-Pourri always grouped several small cartoons with similar themes, which is why part of the big one here has Boston Celtics coach Tom Heinsohn with Jo-jo White and University of Cincinnati athletic director Hindman Wall, along with another Reds drawing of George Foster and Bill Plummer. All about letters.

Cincinnati Enquirer - June 8, 1976

Cincinnati Enquirer - August 3, 1976

Cincinnati Enquirer - June 9, 1976

Cincinnati Enquirer - July 27, 1976

Track stars

It didn't seem to matter what kind of race the Big Red Machine pitchers entered. Whether it was long distance starters or short relief dashes, the staff had the hurling hurdlers up to the task. Seven different pitchers had eleven or more wins, including Alcala, Gary Nolan, Pat Zachry, Fred Norman, Jack Billingham, Don Gullett and relief ace Rawly Eastwick.

And we might as well give credit to the rest of the staff who helped in some way when not playing bullpen basketball — Will McEnaney, Manny Sarmiento, Rich Hinton, Pat Darcy and Joe Henderson.

Opened & shut

Cincinnati Enquirer - August 10, 1976

Cincinnati Enquirer - August 10, 1976

George Foster was having a great year. Johnny Bench, Pete Rose and Joe Morgan had already won the National League MVP award and they were hoping 'Yahtzee' would join the club. George's totals of 29 long balls and 121 runs batted in weren't quite impressive enough to cop the plaque, but he did finish second to — Joe Morgan.

On the mound, rookie ace Pat Zachry closed the lid on the Dodgers and shared the Rookie of the Year award with San Diego Padres closer Butch Metzger.

Closing seasoning

Joe Morgan was adding more than a pinch or a smidgen of seasoning, home runs and RBI's to his already tasty MVP mix. He had runs, walks and stolen bases ready to add, not to mention his batting average. Julia Childs might have asked him for the recipe.

Meanwhile, out in the bullpen, closer Rawly Eastwick was sewing up one save after another.

With the Big Red Machine winning 102 games, Rawly was called on to give sewing lessons to the opponents 71 times, and he stitched together 26 saves with a nifty earned run average of 2.09.

Cincinnati Enquirer - August 31, 1976

Cincinnati Enquirer - September 21, 1976

NATIONAL UE CHAMPIONS

There's a hole in their bucket.....

Cincinnati Enquirer - October 12, 1976

There's a hole in the bucket, dear Phillies, dear Phillies, a hole. Can't fix it, dear Phillies, dear Phillies, dear Phillies etc.

So the song goes by Harry Belafonte, except this version was sung to the Phillies by the Big Red Machine Chorus. There was more than just one hole. The Phillies bucket was shot full of them, some by their own defense, especially a costly error by first baseman Dick "Don't call me Richie" Allen, and the Reds powerful offense.

The BRM boys shot up the Philadelphia bucket with a total of 19 runs in the three game playoff sweep.

The Phillies scored first in all three games, but the Reds poked holes with comeback wins each time, once being three runs down.

Cincinnati Enquirer - October 9, 1976

Beware of the burglars

Phillies manager Danny "Half this game is 90% mental" Ozark, was showing his catcher Bob Boone a photo of what happened to the Pirates during the 1975 playoffs. The Big Red Machine runners had undressed Bucs catcher Manny Sanguillen by running amok on the basepaths and they continued that thievery during the 1976 season.

36 Big Red Versions

As noted at the beginning of this book, the first visual depiction of The Big Red Machine was drawn by this author/artist in 1969. It was also commissioned by the Reds' brass for their 1969 Xmas card.

It was a perfect symbol to illustrate the dominating power of the Reds teams of the 1970s. They won their division six times, the National League title four times, and the World Series twice.

The drawing at the right was used in the Reds 1976 World Series program.

It was so easy to tie the machine concept to different scenarios that the artist used it often.

It must have dawned on the Reds that they could put it to good use by putting a version of it on souvenir buttons, pennants and other products.

Dick Wagner contracted the artist to draw a simple one, which he did, for the princely sum of $75. I probably would have gotten more from Marge Schott.

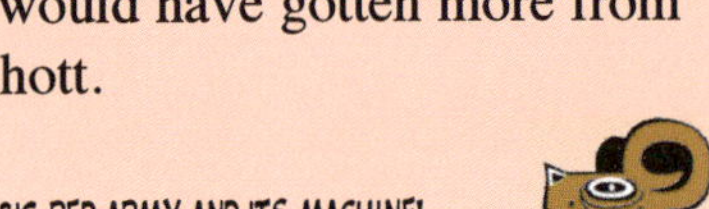

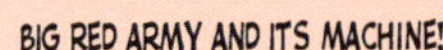

Cincinnati Reds 1976

Photo by Ken Stewart

At a reception held by the Reds in November 1974, this limited edition poster by the great sports cartoonist Willard Mullin was introduced. Cincinnati Post artist Daerick Gross (left) and myself got to chat with Willard at the event. Of course we showed him our samples. Whether or not you can call this depiction a 'machine' is open to question.

Brrrrrrrrr!

Cincinnati Enquirer - October 19, 1976

The Reds were hot but the weather wasn't as the World Series began in freezing Cincinnati. It didn't matter to commissioner Boobie Kuhn, who thought he was vacationing in the deep south. No surprise, as Kuhn's brain was always on vacation.

Just kidding!

Reds pitcher Pat Zachry shared the National League Rookie award with Butch Metzger, while over in the American League Mark "The bird" Fidrych did the same. Zachry didn't talk to the ball the way Fidrych did; his fastball did the yacking!

Cincinnati Enquirer - December 7, 1976

Cincinnati Enquirer - November 30, 1976

Award time!

Joe Morgan's trophy case was getting full with all his awards and titles. The Most Valuable award in 1976 was his second and his Gold Glove award this year was number four. He was Rookie of the Year in 1965 (with Houston).

Moeller High School football coach Gerry Faust yelled and screamed to his way to a few Ohio State titles.

Cincinnati Enquirer - December 5, 1976

$igned with $teinbrenner

After a long contract battle with the Reds, Don Gullett left them and signed with money mad George Steinbrenner; a six year deal for almost two million Yankee bucks.

Bob Howsam had earlier claimed that grabbing free agents like Oakland pitcher Catfish Hunter, and now Gullett meant the end of teams like the Big Red Machine as we know them.

1977

Cincinnati Enquirer - January 30, 1977

Cincinnati Enquirer - January 11. 1977

Full of ... er ... gas?

The guy pouring the budget gas had to deal with players gaseous demands for more fuel, in order to continue gassing up the Big Red Machine.

You'd think they could supply their own, since they seem to be full of it themselves. Rawly Eastwick demanded a huge increase

Cincinnati Enquirer - February 22, 1977

Ad gaseum!

Joe Morgan is one of the greatest at his position, second base, but he is unquestionably the GREATEST at talking about himself!

All one has to do is listen to him on the air during Sunday night baseball with Jon Miller. Every sentence is directed at his knowledge of the game, and he repeats it over and over to make sure the reader gets the message. Ad nauseum! Ad gaseum!

Like the Chinese water torture.

Worse than Joe Garagiola.

Worse than Tim McCarver.

Not quite to the level of Tracy Jones or Doc Rogers, Reds talk blabbers, but he's working on it. Believe me, he'll get there.

This may seem like criticism of Morgan, the present, but in reality he has been gaseous all his career, talking about a 'healthy' Joe Morgan would have done this, or a 'healthy' Joe Morgan would have done that. Blah blah blah and then some more blah!

This cartoon, drawn in 1977, shows that Joe didn't just acquire this self importance recently.

Cincinnati Enquirer - March 13, 1977

Payback!

Cincinnati Enquirer - March 20, 1977

Pay up!

Poor Dick Wagner!

Assigned the task of signing the guys who had two sensational seasons, winning the World Series both in 1975 and 1976, he was trying to keep the payroll down by offering cut rate contracts.

He wasn't able to keep Tony Perez well fed and "Doggie" was swapped to the Montreal Expos for the pitchers Dale Murray and Woodie Fryman.

It was a deal which enraged the local fans who adored Tony.

But Wagner was just beginning to clean house at Riverfront. He became loathed instead of loved.

Cincinnati Enquirer - March 27, 1977

Paycheck!

Rawly Eastwick thought he was a poor homeless waif, residing in the bullpen, which he probably equated to living under a bridge.

He did, however, win eleven games while emerging from his lockup 71 times. He locked up 26 saves for the Big Red Machine in 1976 and wasn't thrilled to be offered a 20% pay cut for 1977.

He was also a workhorse, tossing 106 innings, a huge total for a reliever.

MY HOME IS A HOLE!

Cincinnati Enquirer - April 8, 1977

It may be fashionable these days, but the term 'three-peat' was somewhat unheard of back in the 70's. There was no reason not to expect the Big Red Machine to plow the foe under again in 1977. By sweeping its way through the post season, it was certainly a possibility.

Cincinnati Enquirer - April 22, 1977

Wake up, kiddies!

It was early in the season when the warning signs were appearing.

Whether it was a hangover from the success of the two previous seasons, or they simply had damaged their brains to the point of forgetting the way baseball should be played, it was time to remember that this was new season, and past performances meant absolutely nothing.

Fundamentals were absent. Effort was lacking. Instructions were being ignored. Base running was full of mistakes Everything was affected by the sloppy performance on the field.

Sparky had enough!

He blasted the effort and reminded the guys who was boss and things were going to be done his way. It was back to Anderson Elementary school (or was it kindergarten?) for a refresher course.

Cincinnati Enquirer - April 26, 1977

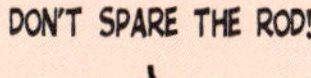

Cincinnati Enquirer - May 3, 1977

Cincinnati Enquirer - June 7, 1977

Not the penguin of Batman fame, but this one was just as dangerous. Especially fond of eating Big Red Meat. This food addiction led to the large belly and was the main cause of the way this bird waddled around his position at third base for the Los Angeles Dodgers.

The comic penguin and the baseball penguin had amazing similarities. They both were arch enemies of batmen — Batman of the comics, and the 'batsmen' of the Big Red Machine.

Baseball's penguin had a name, Ron Cey, who was especially fond of devouring Reds pitchers. He led his team to a big lead early in 1977 and caused Cincinnati exterminators Bench and Foster to go searching for him.

Cincinnati Enquirer - May 3, 1977

The Big Red Machine had quite a few changes from the title teams. In 1977, this bunch was added, led by the great Tom Seaver.

Blasted playoff orbit!

The Dodgers launched their space craft from Los Angeles early in the season. Not from Edwards Air Force base, but Dodger Stadium in Chavez Ravine.

Reds astronauts, led by commander Sparky Anderson, tried to craft a machine which would be capable of intercepting the Dodger ship before it got too far into playoff space.

The harried crew of coaches George Scherger, Russ Nixon, Larry Shepard and Ted Kluszewski tried one design after another. None got off the Riverfront launching pad, and their little rockets tipped over into the Ohio River.

The playoff moon was slowly disappearing into the dark reaches of the 1977 season.

Cincinnati Enquirer - May 10, 1977

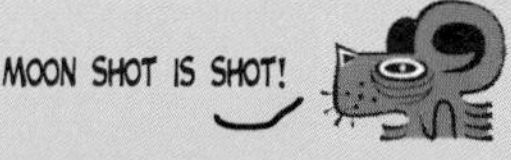

Seaver shadows Stingers!

Cincinnati Enquirer - June 21, 1977

For some reason, John Hewig, the public relations guy with the hockey Cincinnati Stingers, thought that his team was the big news in town.

Not so, when the Reds inked the great Tom Seaver, Hewig went ballistic when I drew the cartoon at left.

Actually, Seaver lasted longer in town than the Stingers four season existence.

Cincinnati Enquirer - June 22, 1977

Cincinnati Enquirer - June 24, 1977

Space recovery

From the Metropolitan area of New York, Tom Seaver docked with a shuttle to planet Cincinnati. His immediate mission was to rescue the Big Red Machine which had become trapped in the tail of the Philadelphia Phillies comet.

If he successfully achieved that difficult task, his jets were turned to complete the journey to the distant Los Angeles Dodgers, who were spinning out of control in the National League Western Division.

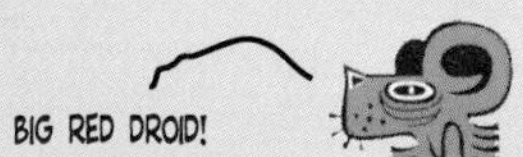

Ups and downs

Up on a chair, afraid of the Big Red Rat giving up huge leads.

Down and off a cliff as the Big Red Machine has come apart, apparently pushed off the pennant road by a runaway Dodger truck.

Representatives of the National League All-Star squad, about to be mugged and knocked down by old foe Martin.

BULLY BILLY!

Cincinnati Enquirer - July 12, 1977

Cincinnati Enquirer - July 19, 1977

Cincinnati Enquirer - August 2, 1977

Thusly, by George!

George Foster had the largest lower jaw in the history of baseball. It could have been used as a bath tub, or a casket. If he came back in another life, he might be a pelican. Thusly (his favorite expression) I drew it that way.

1977 was the year of the home run for George. Thusly he blasted out 52 of them, taking aim at big boys Hack Wilson, Babe Ruth and Roger Maris.

Cincinnati Enquirer - September 1, 1977

Cincinnati Enquirer - August 5, 1977

Cincinnati Enquirer - September 9, 1977

Pheewww!!!

By September, with the Los Angeles Dodgers pulling away to the division title, there was little left of the Big Red Machine and the remains might as well have been left at the curb for the trash collectors to pick up.

Mount Rumpke might have been expanded to accommodate the pile of garbage created by the smelly excuse of a contending team.

The battered Big Red Machine won only 88 games, a drop of twenty from the great team of 1975 and fourteen from the previous year.

As bad as they were this year, they still managed to finish a distant second, ten games behind the Dodgers.

I'M STAYING DOWNWIND!

Cincinnati Enquirer - September 13, 1977

Slobby lobby!

All the Phillies phat boy Greg Luzinski's lobbying did help him, unless you consider finishing second in the voting a success.

George Foster, with his great season, easily copped the award. It was obvious that having a monster season was more impressive to the voters than just being a huge monster.

Just to illustrate what a monster season is, look at these numbers put up by Yahtzee. Average - .320. Home runs - 52. RBI's - 149. Hits - 197. Slugging - .631.

More than Luzinski in every category.

Cincinnati Enquirer - September 17, 1977

Tom Terrific's two hundred!

Future hall of famer Tom Seaver came over to the Reds in mid-season 1977 and finished what he had started in New York with the Mets.

The terrific boy won seven times in New York, then tacked on 14 more with the Reds to win at least twenty for the fifth time.

Seaver won his 200th shortly after joining the Reds and one of the many freelance assignments this artist got from the Reds was to paint '200' on his game ball.

Cincinnati Enquirer - September 24, 1977

Kiss it!

Aptly tagged the "Village Idiot", commish Boobie Kuhn vetoed deals which would have sent ace A's hurler Vida Blue to the Yankees and later the Reds, claiming these were "bad for baseball". He himself was the one "bad for baseball!"

Who's laughing?

To borrow a catch phrase from 'Hockey Bob' Lamey, the play by play announcer for the Indianapolis Racers of the WHA hockey team - "You can pretty much "Kiss this one away!""

That's also pretty much what Sparky was thinking in September as the Reds were kissing the 1977 season away.

Cincinnati Enquirer - December 27, 1977

Cincinnati Enquirer - January 15, 1978

Cincinnati Enquirer - February 1, 1978

Wake up, kiddies!

A twerpy kid named Jimmy Stewart thought he could get away with signing his name, but the real Jimmys discovered his little scam.

And clueless commissioner Boobie Kuhn was just as phony, nixing a deal which would have brought Vida Blue to the Reds.

Tom Seaver was known for dragging his right knee in the dirt on his follow through, and the hole he created by doing so awakened the gopher, who then emerged, saw Tom's shadow, and promised six more months of gopher balls. Seaver the gopher guy, finished the 1978 season with 26 of them. That would be an ordinary month for today's gopher master Aaron Harang.

BOYS WILL BE DIRTY BOYS!

Another Tommy, LaSorda of the Dodgers, got his face and belly dragged in the sand.

Cincinnati Enquirer - April 28,1978

Cincinnati Enquirer - June 13, 1978

1978 The Big Red Four!

Cincinnati Enquirer - July 2, 1978

Cincinnati Enquirer - July 4, 1978

The Enquirer published a series of the present best at each major league position. To nobody's surprise, the Big Red Machine placed four of their stars on this team of 1978 type greats. Where's Pete? Well, he wasn't exactly great at third base. Two of these players are in the Hall of Fame, as would Concepcion if he had played in New York.

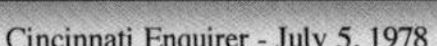

Cincinnati Enquirer - July 5, 1978

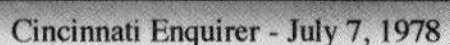

Cincinnati Enquirer - July 7, 1978

Rookie driver in the seat

Cincinnati Enquirer - May 16, 1978

Cincinnati Enquirer - July 25, 1978

The National League West race was usually between two teams, if you can call the runaway 1975 and 1976 seasons actual races. This year, however, a late qualifier appeared out of nowhere, and challenged the Reds and Dodgers. Second year manager Joe Altobelli took the wheel and steered his San Francisco Giants onto the lead lap for a while.

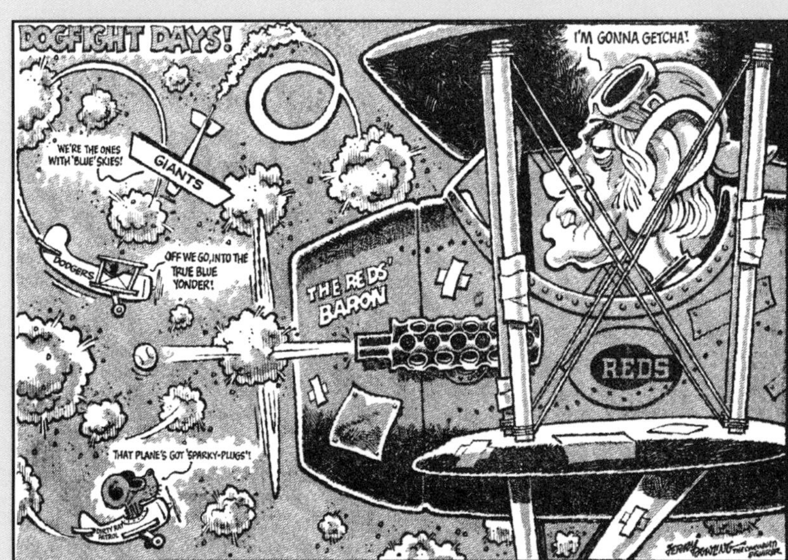

Cincinnati Enquirer - August 8, 1978

Cincinnati Enquirer - August 22, 1978

Big Red Baron

Dog fight! Fist fight! Rat fight! Whatever you want to call the 1978 season, it was the main event for a long time. A lot of it was fought in the air, machine gun type home runs and grand slam bombs. The Big Red Baron had to deal with two enemies, both out to shoot him down. Sparky Anderson might have gotten in touch with the other famous Sparky, Peanuts cartoonist Charles Schulz and borrow Snoopy, who was also involved frequently in these aerial battles.

As the 1978 season progressed, there were still the same three battle squads going at it. Late August — and the Reds, Dodgers and Giants all thought they were going to emerge victorious. It was getting bloody. Both Sparky Anderson and Tommy LaSorda were battle scarred while Joe Altobelli was still learning the ropes.

Ballroom dancer

Lucy's in the Sky newsletter , 1978

The Reds of 1978 were worse than mediocre, so even mediocre outfielder Ken Henderson was an improvement. Or so they thought. He questionably was injured, but not enough to go dancing. Most of his scoring was at the downtown club, 'Lucy's in the Sky'. His average there had to be higher than his baseball number that year, .167.

Classic restoration

General manager Dick Wagner thought that by tearing down the Big Red Machine, he could then rebuild a new model which would be more powerful than the previous one.

He had discarded, one way or another, vital parts Pete Rose, Joe Morgan and Tony Perez. Not to mention canning the head mechanic, Sparky Anderson. Little did he realize how much damage he created doing so.

Assigned to put the damaged parts together with a few new ones was former Oakland A's manager John McNamara, who had experience with nuts, having worked for owner Charlie Finley.

Cincinnati Enquirer - December 10, 1978

Cincinnati Enquirer - March 6, 1979

1979 Who caught who?

Taking the bait, George "Yahtzee" Foster landed a big contract from the fisherboy Wagner. It was difficult to figure who really got hooked, but it probably was Dick, the head honcho with the worms.

The muscular fish bit on a three year deal, hooked on for $750,000 per season.

After tossing most of his older fish, including Pete Rose, Joe Morgan, Tony Perez, Ken Griffey, Cesar Geronimo and Dave Collins into the baseball waters, Wagner had to fill the Reds creel again. The only thing he caught at first was grief from the fans.

Once landed, Foster declared that he wanted to finish his career with the Reds. He didn't.

Picture this!

Cincinnati Enquirer - March 17, 1979

Fictitious newspaper photographer F. Stop Fitzgerald had a shorter career than former Reds pitcher Steve Blateric, and nobody heard of him either. But he did shoot local events and teams for a little more than a year. Here he is taking a shot of new Reds manager John McNamara who was busy changing the image of the Big Red Machine to his liking.

Cincinnati Enquirer - May 1, 1979

Why picture this?

Cincinnati Enquirer - May 8, 1979

Champ Summers was a utility player for three seasons, mainly as a backup right fielder and pinch hitter. He amassed the grand total of five home runs and had a Reds batting average of .193.

Pedro Borbon was a relief hurler and designated biter. They must have had a good game together once, deserving of a cartoon. I can't think of any other reason to draw one about those two.

Space shot

Spinning out of control early in the 1979 season was the Astrolab which had been launched from the space center in Houston.

Fearing damage from outer space, George Foster took it upon himself to fly up there and thusly capture it with the intent of either blowing it up with a huge power show or send it back to earth where it couldn't cause any more problems.

Fire when not ready!

After nine years with Anderson as the head mechanic, general manager Dick Wagner made an extremely unpopular move, firing Sparky and bringing in rather unknown John McNamara to fix the Big Red Machine.

John McNamara

Cincinnati Enquirer - April 4, 1979

This is the 1979 Reds Yearbook cover, commissioned by Reds.

For some reason 'Gumby', as Reds publications director Bob Rathgeber was known, wrote in the book's credits that the artist's father sang a song called 'McNamara's Band' to him as a child, when in fact, he had never heard of either the song or John McNamara.*

*Actually, he did hear about both the song and McNamara, but claiming not to makes for a better story!

Cincinnati Reds Yearbook - 1979

Tommy gun and pop gun

Tommy LaSorda goes gunning for new Reds mentor John McNamara, since his Los Angeles Dodgers seem to have taken over the National League from the Big Red Machine, winning the pennant the previous two years. Mac is more than ready for the battle of 1979.

Phillies Fhat manager Danny Ozark can't believe that George Foster can pop all those long balls into the seats so he makes up this ridiculous charge that Yahtzee is filling his pop guns with cork.

Cincinnati Enquirer - May 18, 1979

Cincinnati Enquirer - December 9, 1979

Cincinnati Enquirer - June 5, 1979

Job search

With his career on the downswing following a couple mediocre years, Joe Morgan decided to test the market. The once speedy little guy was granted his release and he started shopping.

He found out that he wasn't exactly the hot commodity he thought and was nixed by several teams before eventually signing with the Houston Astros, back where it all began in 1963.

1980 Hit these signs-win!

Dick's tricky pitches weren't fooling a couple of his players as he attempted to dust them. Dave Collins and Ray Knight had seen his pitch selection before and they were laying off his low ball offerings. Both players hit Wagner's soft tosses and won their arbitration games.

Cincinnati Enquirer - February 10, 1980

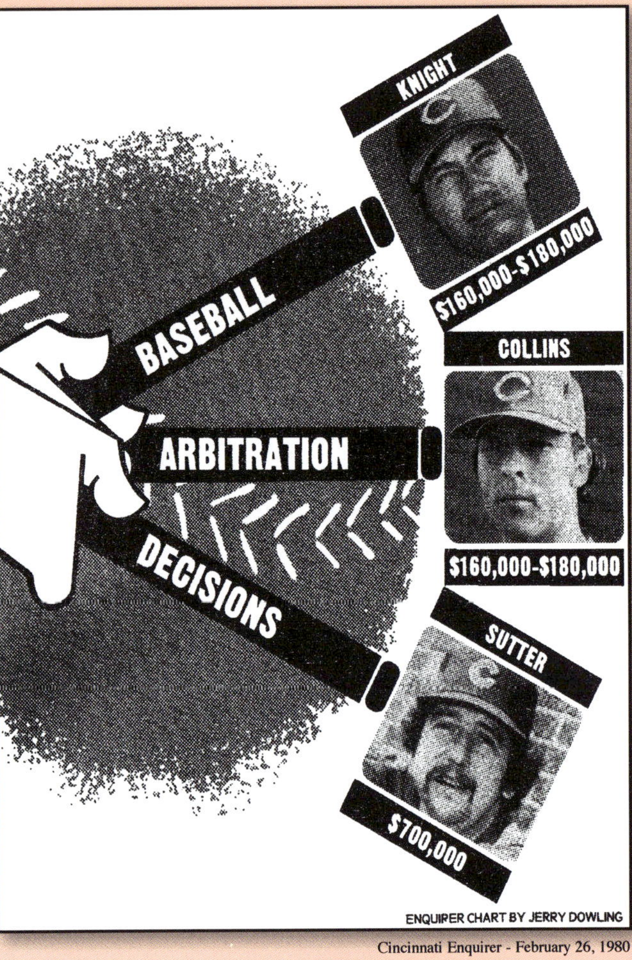

Cincinnati Enquirer - February 26, 1980

Swallow these!

The defending National League West champion Reds began the 1980 season 'Reds hot!' by letting the San Francisco Giants and Atlanta Braves eat samples from their Riverfront food stand.

Even though Cincinnati was noted for its fiery chili chow, this twenty-five way grub was hotter still, with a 7-0 start at home before taking the Big Red Food Cart on the road and winning four out of the next five.

Braves manager Bobby Cox, in his first stint with that team, and former Reds skipper Dave Bristol, now the boss of the Giants, were the designated testers of Mac's offerings. Both choked and wondered what could be so throat challenged.

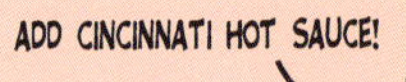

Cincinnati Enquirer - April 20, 1980

Knuckled down and out!

Opening day 1980. Second inning. George Foster the batter. Phil Niekro the Braves starting pitcher. Knuckleball thrown. BASH! Home Run!
Thusly, a message sent!

Cincinnati Enquirer - April 9, 1980

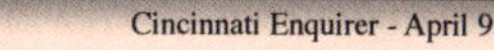

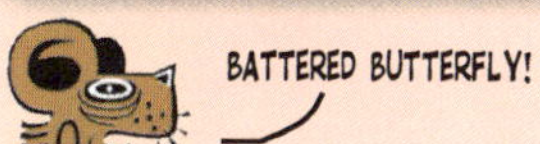

Cincinnati Enquirer -April, 1980

And then...

After the terrific 12-2 start of the season, everything went south all of a sudden. Starting with a bad trip west (an affliction the Reds have to this day), they quickly lost seven of eight and dropped into second place, 2 1/2 games behind the Chicago Cubs, although being behind the Windy City Flubbies is never a cause for panic.

Cincinnati Enquirer - April 1980

Cincinnati Enquirer - July 6, 1980

Piecing it together

With the season approaching the half way point, the Reds were still a puzzle. They were in third place, but still within striking distance of the lead. Many pieces were either missing or didn't fit properly.

George Foster's bat was lost somewhere and thusly his power numbers were not to be located.

Tom Seaver's winning right arm mysteriously disappeared while another pitcher, Mike LaCoss, went looking for some triumphant parts himself.

Johnny Bench's pieces had frayed edges.

Hurler Bill Bonham was never even in the box. His season and career ended that July.

Cincinnati Enquirer - August 17, 1980

Short trip!

The day this cartoon ran, the Reds had made it back up to first place and had just won in Los Angeles. Maybe it was a jinx, but the lead lasted as long as the days' newspaper, which then became a fish wrap or a bird cage liner.

The Big Red Fargo depicted here was scheduled for a far trip to the playoffs, but there were still quite a few obstacles in the road.

Bespectacled catcher Joe Nolan, being groomed as the heir apparent for Johnny Bench, was part of this mail team of young horses which included infielder Ron Oester and pitchers Mario Soto and Paul Moskau.

Cincinnati Enquirer - September 7, 1980

Server Seaver

It took until late in the season for server Tom Seaver to deliver the Western Division victory meals with consistency.

Customer McNamara, expecting faster service, had already donned his playoff bib and had his utensils ready to dig in. He was famished.

Once his main course finally arrived, he had to eat in a hurry before the food was gone. The other contenders had already begun and it might just be leftovers for the Reds manager.

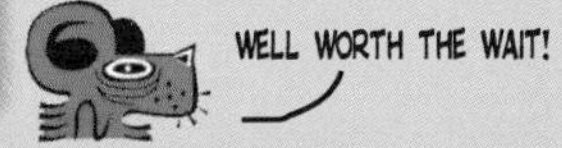

Pest!

In spite of having problems with some of the big guys having off years, McNamara had his team deep into the September playoff hunt.

Dodgers manager Tommy LaSorda and Astros boss Bill Virdon were sweating and couldn't concentrate on their own battle as long as McNamara was still being a nuisance.

Cincinnati Enquirer - September 15, 1980

All about the money

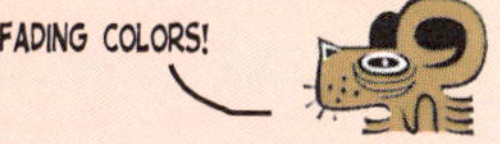

The season on the field was over, with the Big Red Machine stalling in September. It was left sitting helpless at the side of the road. General manager Dick Wagner now had the task of getting enough help to put it back on the highway of contention. Every place he looked for cheap help came up empty.

Meanwhile, All-Star catcher Johnny Bench himself tried to negotiate with Wagner, and his demands were a wash, but his demand paint wasn't washable.

Cincinnati Enquirer - November 13, 1980

1981

Cincinnati Enquirer - February 18, 1981

BIG BILL!

Fellow press box minion, Bill "BIG" Staubitz published a newsletter called "PRESSBOX NEWSLETTER" for a couple years. He got a few of his associates to participate by each writing pieces. Caricatures of Hal McCoy, Bob Hertzel, Mike Lopresti, Skip Korb, Joe Minster and Big Bill himself went with each of their columns. Quite a roster. The artist didn't draw himself. "BIG" paid the entire staff out of his own pocket, but his pocket had holes in it.

Pressbox Newsletter - May 14, 1980

Pressbox Newsletter - June 4, 1980

Pressbox Newsletter - June 25, 1980

Pressbox Newsletter - July 16, 1980

Pressbox Newsletter - August 6, 1980

Pressbox Newsletter - August 27, 1980

Pressbox Newsletter - September 24, 1980

Pressbox Newsletter - October 15, 1980

Pressbox Newsletter - January 2, 1981

Pressbox Newsletter - April 24, 1981

Pressbox Newsletter - May 15, 1981

Pressbox Newsletter - March 27, 1981

Here are a few of the PRESSBOX NEWSLETTER cartoons. One in particular, made fun of George Foster being afraid of crashing the wall, which upset Skip Korb to the point that he quit writing for us.

DIDN'T PAY ME!

Most of the questions manager John McNamara faced had been already answered with the signings of several holdover holdouts.

The one remaining question (and a HUGE one!) for McNamara was what catcher to pencil in on his lineup card. Actually, Mac would rather have used ink instead of pencil to enter Bench's name.

But the greatest catcher known to mankind was threatening free agency. This left a selection of Joe Nolan and Mike O'Berry. Nolan had to be favored to wear the 'tools of ignorance', having hit over .300 in limited time with the Reds in 1980, while lighter hitting catcher (lifetime average of .191) Mike O'Berry came over from the Chicago Cubs.

Cincinnati Enquirer - March 8, 1981

Cincinnati Enquirer - February 5, 1981

Mixologist

Center fielder Dave Collins was using his 1980 numbers - 79 stolen bases, 94 runs, 167 hits and a .303 average in 144 games as a basis for negotiating a new contract, although he was accused of padding the stolen base mark by turning doubles into singles to have better chances at swiping more bags.

Cincinnati Enquirer - April 7, 1981

ENQUIRER BASEBALL '81

WEDNESDAY, APRIL 8, 1981

REDS

SEAVER 41

Cincinnati Enquirer - April 8, 1981

New faces, new decade

New faces not normally associated with what we know as the Big Red Machine shown on this illustration are pitchers Frank Pastore and Tom Hume, and infielders Ray Knight and Dan Driessen.

Sir Walksalot

Slick fielding first sacker Danny Driessen was also a better than average hitter who walked a lot. He led the league in free passes in 1980, with 93.

This was before the intentional walk days of Barry Bonds and Albert Pujols.

Cincinnati Enquirer - April 9, 1981

Cincinnati Enquirer - August 9, 1981

Big Red Catcher

Johnny Bench was the all around athlete. As well known as he was with the bat, he was just plain amazing the way he handled his big catcher's mitt. Whether it was climbing the fence to snag a foul ball, or making a gloved sweep tag at the plate, he was something to behold.

Big Green Grabber

Another big catch was made by Dave Concepcion, the glove master shortstop, this time catching big money, with advice from leech agent Jerry Kapstein.

Maybe the moon wasn't that far off into space, as Davey and negotiator Kapstein upped the 1982 paycheck from the $200,000 Reds annual pittance to a five year deal of $4.6 million.

Cincinnati Enquirer - October 4, 1981

Baseball '82

THE CINCINNATI ENQUIRER
Monday April 5.1982

Tom Seaver

Cincinnati Enquirer - April 5, 1982

Nice cover... but...

Reds ace Tom Seaver had been announced as the 1982 Opening Day starter long before, so we felt very confident that we could feature his image on *The Enquirer's* Special Section cover.

Nothing is guaranteed, and Seaver came down sick that morning and couldn't pitch.

Of all the people to run into in the press box that afternoon, it had to be my friend, former Bengals star and present TV commentator Bob Trumpy. He wasted no time informing me that it was a great drawing, but "At least you got the uniform right!"

Tom's replacement happened to be Mario Soto, whose start began a streak of five consecutive Opening Day starts and added another one later for a total of six, a team record approached recently by Aaron Harang.

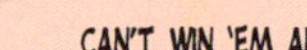

Upsetting Upsets!

On Opening Day 1982, both home plate umpire John Kibler and Reds manager John McNamara were upset — with each other! In the pouring rain, McNamara was invited to make use of this rain water to take a shower with a brush and soap. Kibler was so proud of himself that he requested this cartoon original. I flushed it down the drain to the umpires dressing room.

The alleged favorite Reds started the season by going 3-10 while the brave little Atlanta Braves, upset the division bucket, by winning their first 13 games. They poured a huge division sand lead over the Reds head, which included smashing five straight Reds sand piles.

It was upsetting to see the National League West standings listed upside down by May. Perennial bottom feeders Atlanta Braves were in reverse, at the top. The Reds, who, even with the best over all record, had been shafted in the strike screwed split season of 1981. They were the favorites to cop the title this year.

Cincinnati Enquirer - April 6, 1982

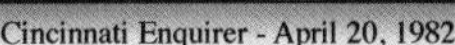

Cincinnati Enquirer - April 20, 1982

Cincinnati Enquirer - May 4, 1982

Cincinnati Enquirer - May 21, 1982

Punch pound 62*?

The Reds' early season power numbers were so anemic that it was looking more and more that the whole team might not even challenge Roger Maris' asterisk record of 61, set in 1961.

That asterisk was awarded by another ineffective commissioner at the time, Ford Frick.

Just to poke fun with the Reds lack of home runs, I figured that the master of indecision, commissioner Bowie Kuhn would nervously tack an asterisk onto the Reds in the case they hit number 62 for the year.

If telephones had punch numbers in 1982, Bowie would've had a field day with *************'s.

Heavy load

Danny Driessen tried his best to lift the Reds to decency in 1982, but he wasn't the huge power hitter the locals were used to. He led the sorry squad with a mere 17 homers.

Cincinnati Enquirer - June 8, 1982

Cincinnati Enquirer - May 25, 1982

Storm warning

Dangerous offensive weather seemed to be on the horizon but the hitting storms kept passing over the Reds early in the season.

The drought lasted all year and the team finished with an unbelievably low total of 82 long balls, topped by first baseman Danny Driessen's 17. That team number was only nine more than one man, the San Francisco Giants' Barry Bonds, slammed years later.

At least the Reds weren't investigated for steroids.

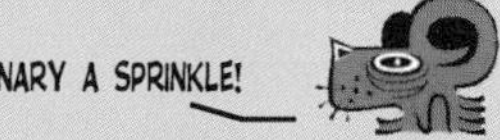

Cincinnati Enquirer - June 29, 1982

Nothing to like!

Whatever the Reds individual numbers read - they all add up to this one - zero!

Once the ace of the pitching staff Tom Seaver had the worst year of his career, going 5-13. The top hurler was Mario Soto, the only one on the staff over .500, with a 14-13 record.

Remember Bruce Berenyi? He won nine. Remember Bob Shirley? He won eight. No? Well, those two followed Soto in total victories.

Some of the power outage was caused by the trade of George Foster to The New York Mets in February.

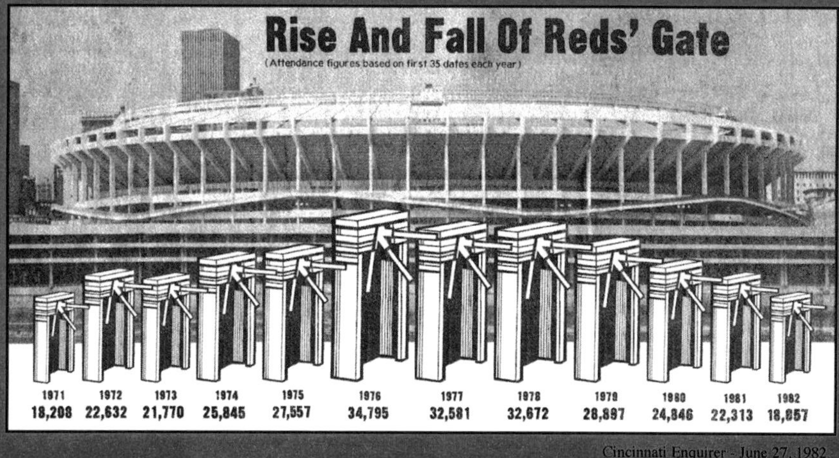

Cincinnati Enquirer - June 27, 1982

What's up comes down

The novelty of having a legitimate contending team and a new ball park wore off gradually as the numbers indicated.

Cincinnati Enquirer - July 8, 1982

Battered banner

The Reds season was rapidly sinking to dismal depths. Desperate Dick was worrying that he wouldn't have to edit the flag which was once proudly displayed atop Riverfront Stadium, but the day of doom was arriving in July as the Minnesota Twins were emerging from the American League West dungeon and might drop the former Big Red Machine into the Major League cellar.

To go from first to worst in just a few months was an achievement that was not only totally unexpected but disheartening to the fans, and attendance at home dropped as much as the won-loss record.

WE'RE FEELING LOW!

Reds Worst In League

Page C-1

Eating away

PAC-MAN was a popular monster eating game. MAC-MAN was an unpopular manager eating game. With the Reds dropping into the basement, it was inevitable that general manager Dick Wagner's eating game would be the contract of John McNamara.

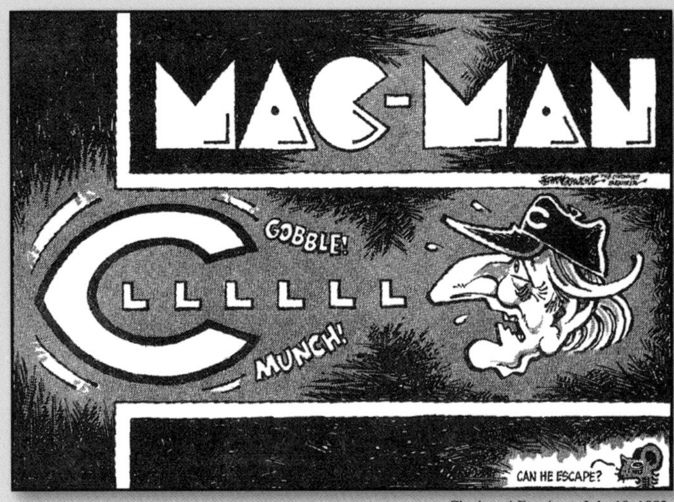

Cincinnati Enquirer - July 10, 1982

Cincinnati Enquirer - July 20, 1982

Up in arms

No relation! A Nixon returns! Not the deposed President Richard, but former Major League catcher Russ Nixon, a Cincinnati native, was coming back home to manage the Reds.

Another Richard, the Wagner one, deposed John McNamara after the Reds sorry start of the 1982 season. Rumors had it that Gerald Ford turned down the job.

Russ did even worse than his predecessor, leading his forces to only 27 wins of the remaining 70 games.

The Reds commissioned the artist to draw the cartoon below for their Reds-Letter publication, hoping to give the fans some semblance of hope.

Nixon had no previous experience at the job, and he only lasted until the end of the 1983 season, with a woeful record of 101-131 during his term at Riverfront. He was replaced by the loveable Vern Rapp.

'V' WASN'T FOR VICTORY!

Cincinnati Enquirer - July 22, 1982

Reds- Letter, 1982

Cincinnati Enquirer - August 12, 1982

Making the Cut

John McNamara soon had more company in the ocean bottom when the Pittsburgh Pirates cut manager Bill Virdon. Number six.

Flaky pitcher Jim "the emu" Kern was ordered to shave. Resisting, he himself was cut, sent to the Chicago White Sox for 'TBA".

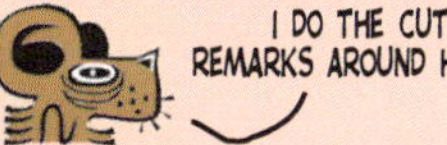

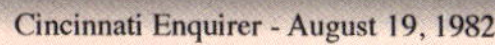
Cincinnati Enquirer - August 19, 1982

Cincinnati Enquirer - August 29, 1982

Hairy situation

Following the rules established by Bob Howsam, general manager Wagner insisted that there be absolutely no facial hair. No mustaches, beards or long hair. That policy held true until the Reds in later years allowed new signee Greg Vaughn to keep his goatee, and of course, owner Marge Schott also kept her whiskers.

Fire sale!

This may be my favorite page in this entire book. The '582' cartoon pretty much sums up the entire debacle of the 1982 season. Even the Reds mascot was ashamed of what transpired on the field for six months of alleged major league baseball. Dick Wagner's deals led to the total destruction of what was formerly the Big Red Machine. The only things red remaining were the embarrassed faces of the loyal fans.

Cincinnati Enquirer - September 23, 1982

Cincinnati Enquirer - October 4, 1982

Cincinnati Enquirer - November 1, 1982

Cincinnati Enquirer - November 14, 1982

Cincinnati Enquirer - November 28, 1982

Wishful thinking

Big changes were in order for the team that lost 101 games in 1982.

Unloading worn out pitcher Tom Seaver was top priority and general manager Dick Wagner was taking offers. All he could get were — try to remember these names, if possible — Charlie Puleo, Jason Felice and Lloyd McClendon from the New York Mets who were hoping Seaver would return to his former greatness by coming home to Shea Stadium.

The re-entry draft that assistant general manager Woody Woodward was sent to was just that – a cold draft.

The winter meetings were held in Hawaii and Wagner danced around with dreams of swaying a few deals to fill the Reds serious power holes with attractive pickups Bob Horner, Jack Clark or Buddy Bell. His dream was all wet.

Cincinnati Enquirer - December 9, 1982

Manhattan!

Cincinnati Enquirer - December 14, 1982

The Big Apple! - First in everything, including shooting, mugging, littering, vandalism and especially subway graffiti! Even the huge baseball bat which stood at the old Yankee Stadium was sprayed and defaced with moronic graffiti as high as the local thugs could reach.

Tom, as in 'Tom Terrific', had become somewhat unterrific in 1982, and he parted company with the Reds following the season. Possibly because his 5-13 won-loss record, along with an equally squalid 5.50 earned run average, his performance on the mound resembled Manhattan graffiti slime, he became a natural fit to return to the house of rotten apples.

The homecoming party didn't do much to improve his numbers, and he was gone from New York after one season.

This cartoon ranks high on the list of the author's favorites in this book.

Madman!

Cincinnati Enquirer - February 20, 1983

1983

If one can imagine asking for a big salary increase after a 9-18 1982 season mark, Bruce Berenyi is your man. His pitch might have been good, but nothing else was.

The Reds tried all sorts of marketing tricks to bump up attendance, such as a variety of hat color combinations.

Madhatrack!

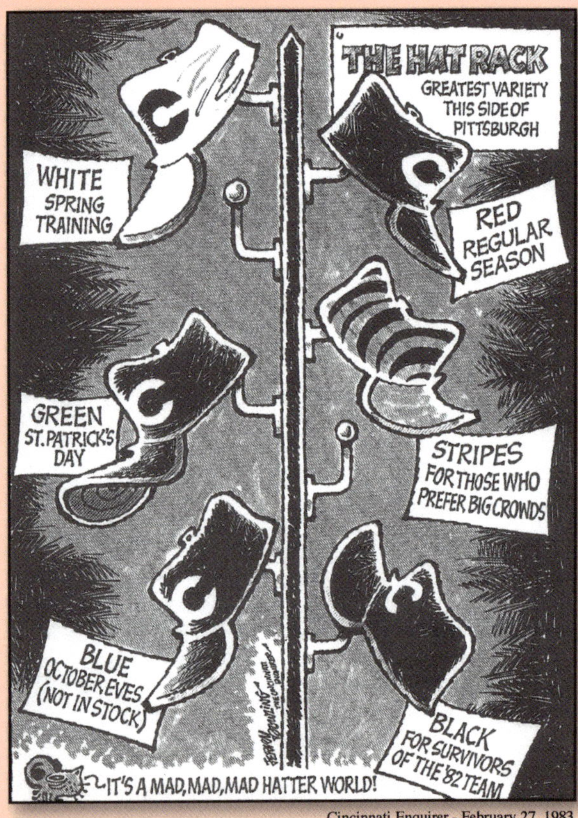

Cincinnati Enquirer - February 27, 1983

Open season

Cincinnati Enquirer - March 29, 1983

Catcher Alex Trevino was the heir apparent to Johnny Bench, whose shoes were obviously too big for little Alex to fill, as were his bat and glove. Pitchers had problems with the way he called their pitches and complained openly.

Cincinnati Enquirer - March 20, 1983

Seasoned poker player?

General manager Dick Wagner always thought he was just as great a card manipulator as his predecessor Bob Howsam.

Not quite so! The difference was that Trader Bob played high stakes poker and almost always cleaned up the pot, while Wags, whom many thought he played without a full deck, usually lost simple little kiddie style games.

Opening the season!

Huge hurler Brad 'The Animal' Lesley had a mouth to match his 6'6" stature. Most of his short tenure with the Reds organization was spent in the minors, where he developed his loudmouth act. His transportation to AAA Indianapolis was a bus, a tad slower than the race cars could see from his motel window at Indy.

He could have served as the model for today's National Basketball Association hot dogs.

USED AN AAA MAP!

Cincinnati Enquirer - April 3, 1983

Gary Wallbanger!
On 1983 Opening Day, Redus had a ball, slamming both it and the center field wall.

Cincinnati Enquirer - April 5, 1983

Cincinnati Enquirer - May 2, 1983

The other Nixon

The only similarity between the infamous Richard Nixon and the unfamous Russ Nixon is that they were both on the right, the tricky one being a right wing Republican, and the Reds skipper being on the right side of this page.

After asking for better sneakers, manager Russ was handed the necessary speedy footwear acquisitions in Paul Householder, Gary Redus, Cesar Cedeno, Eddie Milner and Ron Oester.

Now that the Reds team speed was vastly improved, another major problem popped up. Too many of the pitchers were getting bombed with regularity. Manager Russ was doing his level best to detonate these bombs before his team bombed out of the race. Tom Hume, Rich Gale, Frank Pastore and Charlie Puleo were the main duds.

THE 'N' BOMB!

Cincinnati Enquirer - May 17, 1983

Cincinnati Enquirer - May 24, 1983

This seat's taken!

Right field had been occupied on a regular basis by Cesar Cedeno in 1982. The Reds brought Cedeno in from the Houston Astros, hoping he still had some gas left for the Machine tank. For the former All-Star and Gold Glove performer, only a few drips remained.

1983 saw Cedeno's aging statistics fall significantly. Second year Red, Paul Householder assisted in unseating him from the right field position.

Cedeno regained the spot later and played a couple more fairly decent seasons with the Reds, St. Louis Cardinals and Los Angeles Dodgers.

Householder never lived up to his household name, bouncing around until 1987, with a final lifetime batting average of .236.

FROM THE CHAIR TO THE BENCH!

Davey in the dark

With the pending retirement of the great Johnny Bench at the end of the 1983 season, only veteran shortstop Dave Concepcion remained from the nucleus of the Big Red Machine teams

Cincinnati Enquirer - June 12, 1983

Cincinnati Enquirer - July 31, 1983

Big Black Bootsies!

Assistant general manager Woody Woodward, following the good old company line, insisted that the players wear plain black spikes.

No way, said rebellious pitcher Frank Pastore, who was a winner in the players grievance filed against the owners. He and others could pocket a little royalty cash by wearing logo laden footsies!

Starry days and nights

Every year at summer's end, Cincinnati celebrates the finale by putting on a spectacular fireworks display on the Ohio River adjacent to the ballpark.

In 1983, the Reds seemed to end their season early (some say mid April was when it ended) and celebrated by shooting up a small sparkler which fizzled immediately.

If Marge Schott had been the owner then, she wouldn't have needed to worry about fireworks cost.

Cincinnati Enquirer - September 4, 1983

Cincinnati Enquirer - August 14, 1983

Hi there!

Bob 'Hi there!' Howsam, the 70s version of Tony LaRussa (aka 'genius'), was lured out of retirement to see what he could do as far as saving the Big Red Machine from further disgrace and distress. Its color had faded to a dull, splotchy pink and was in serious need of a shiny new finish.

Cincinnati Enquirer - October 6, 1983

Round two

A well known fact about Trader Bob Howsam was that he was a seldom beaten fighter. Starting with being a U.S. Navy pilot in World War II to being one of the American Football League challengers, he would back down from nobody.

Here he is depicted delivering a knuckle sandwich to Reds manager Russ Nixon.

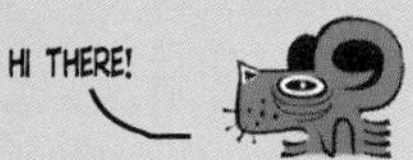

Grave situation!

Digging out of the hole created by players retiring and moving on elsewhere became a task too deep for poor Russ Nixon to accomplish, and he was buried after the 1983 season.

He must have gotten used to the baseball cemetery, as his second managerial stint, in Atlanta, produced the same last place results.

...A...A...LIGHT?

'70's GOLD MINE

NIXON

COLLAPSE OF '82

EARLY '83

BUT YOU STILL HAVE TO GET OUT OF HERE!

Cincinnati Enquirer - September 20, 1983

Balanced diet

Pedro Borbon made sure he ate properly - meat, proteins, fibers...

Cincinnati Enquirer - November 4, 1983

Hairy deal

Not by the hair on his chinny chin chin was Parker allowed in (to the Reds house).

So signed as free agent, Dave had to shave off his beard, but he also was able to discard the ridiculous Pittsburgh uniform combinations.

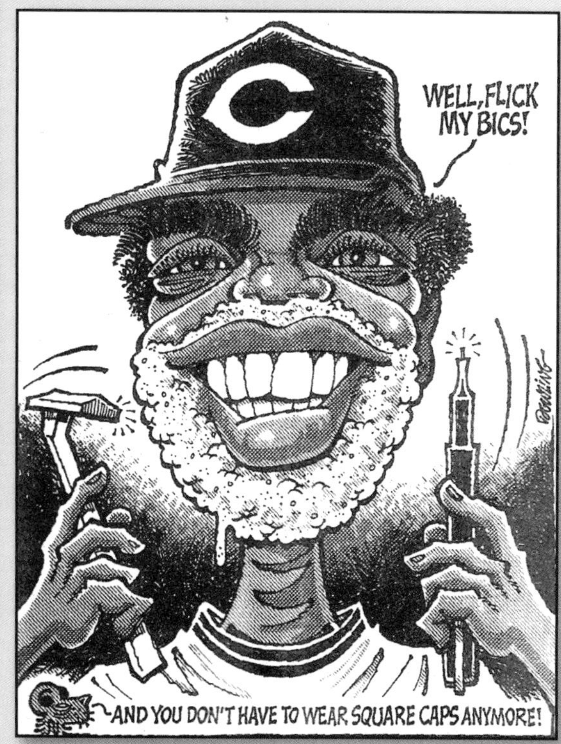

Cincinnati Enquirer - December 8, 1983

1984

Cincinnati Enquirer - April 2, 1984

Change for the Strange! Strange!

Above are newcomers Dave Parker, a huge power hitting former National League Most Valuable Player, and Mr. Personality, new manager Vern Rapp, along with Trader Bob Howsam.

Instead of 1984 being the season of change, it became the season of strange.

It was a year full of suspensions and brawls, while new owner Marge Schott engineered the return of Pete Rose as player manager, which led to the early departure of Vern Rapp in August.

You'll see drawing depictions of these momentous events in pages following.

Cincinnati Enquirer - April 3, 1984

Going bats!

The Opening Day game was won by the Reds with the help of unlikely bashers Eddie Milner and Dave Concepcion.

Those two slim sluggers each hit a home run to lead the home team to an 8-1 whipping of the New York Mets. It was their only victory in the first four games of the season.

It's too bad this power show didn't last much longer as Concepcion hit only three more and Milner added six the rest of the 1984 season.

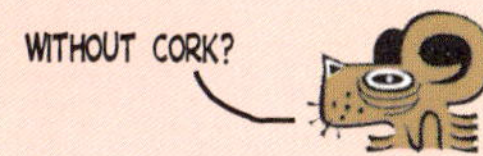

Three's a company?

Here is a triptych of baseball brain-a-like boys.

Reds skipper Vern Rapp had a file on Dave Parker's missing home runs. Boobie Kuhn bravely banned a Brave and Boss George was about to axe Billy Martin — Again!

Cincinnati Enquirer - May 6, 1984

Cincinnati Enquirer - May 25, 1984

Boomball 84! 84!

Reds reliever Tom Hume (later, for some reason, the pitching coach), had a horrible penchant for feeding the gophers that hung around the mound.

Cincinnati Enquirer -June 8, 1984

Last one standing

Of all the important pieces of the Big Red Machine teams of the 70s, shortstop Dave Concepcion was the only remaining part.

Catcher Johnny Bench, second sacker Joe Morgan and first baseman Tony Perez are members of baseball's Hall of Fame in Cooperstown, as are manager Sparky Anderson and announcer Marty Brennaman. Third baseman Pete Rose would be there except for a slight problem with the bookies.

Dave Concepcion has had this writer's vote every year, having witnessed the greatness of the guy on the field as well as wielding a pretty damn good bat.

The other regulars — outfielders Ken Griffey, Cesar Geronimo and George Foster weren't too far off from being in the shrine themselves.

Cincinnati Enquirer - July 6, 1984

The original draw(n) bridge

Reds ace Mario Soto had a temper management problem in 1984, resulting in his being reprimanded more than once by National League President Chub Feeney. His main combatant was Claudell Washington of the Atlanta Braves.

Unabridged Soto

This from *Sports Illustrated,* July 23, 1984: "Jerry Dowling, a cartoonist for the *Enquirer*, drew Soto sitting atop a Cincinnati bridge known, ironically enough, as the Suspension Bridge. Soto is depicted reading a letter — "Dear Mario, Your recent request for a name change to Soto Low Bridge is hereby denied. Also, the Washington Bridge referred to is named after George, not Claudell. Love, Chub."

Hi there etc.......

Players leaving! Players arriving! Up the DOWN escalator! Down the UP escalator! In the door! Out the door! Hi there! Bye there!

General manager Trader Bob Howsam, brought back to serve a second term by Marge Schott, hopefully to rebuild a worn out Big Red Machine.

The biggest deal Howsam pulled off upon his return was getting little used Pete Rose from the Montreal Expos in exchange for of little use Tom Lawless.

Maybe it was this coup that renewed fan interest in the Reds, suffering from poor field performance and attendance to match, that Bob felt his mission was accomplished, and he retired for good after the season.

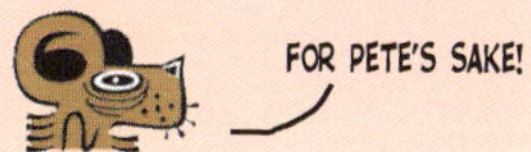

Cincinnati Enquirer - July 12, 1984

Cincinnati Enquirer - July 24, 1984

Cheapshots?

"Who's this Dowling guy?", the subject of this drawing asked.

Well, this guy happens to be the villain who drew the cartoon here which upset manager Vern Rapp. All the bad guy did was to portray the inept leader the way he saw it, and the way many others did. I can only assume that I'd have been a target, verbally or physically, of the beloved Rapp crap. This kind of reaction is exactly why this artist seldom went into dressing rooms for quotes or reactions to questionable situations on the field. My intention always is to portray what I see in a satirical and funny way. Some athletes understand that, while others unfortunately, don't. Nor did owner Marge Schott. Surprisingly, general manager Dick Wagner always saw humor in the cartoons, and he got hammered pretty good.

Fellow *Enquirer* cohort, Reds beat writer Greg Hoard once proclaimed that he was ready for any level of abuse in his job, now that he had survived Vern Rapp's diatribes.

Cincinnati Enquirer - August 16, 1984

The Spark plug!

More important than the chance to get rid of manager Vern Rapp (but not much) was the opportunity to return the beloved Pete Rose to his home turf.

Rose had become a part time performer for the Montreal Expos and he wasn't going to get enough at bats to accumulate the necessary hits there to replace Ty Cobb as baseball's all-time hit king.

By being player manager of the Reds, Pete could insert himself in the lineup on a regular basis at first base. True to form, he singled and later dove into third his first time back a Red.

The Reds didn't exactly give up much in this deal, costing them only utility infielder Tom Lawless.

PETE KNOWS TURF!

To the rescue!

Or she claimed!

Marge saved the city from losing the Reds and other assorted fables!

The team was never in serious trouble of leaving the city, but Marge Schott claimed to be the savior when she bought controlling shares for a paltry $13,000,000.

Maybe she thought the Big Red Machine was another car running on treads instead of tires.

She didn't like this portrayal of her as a St. Bernard rescuing animal.

Cincinnati Enquirer - December 22, 1984

Cincinnati Enquirer - February 10, 1985

1985

Didn't take long!

In February 1981, erstwhile car dealer Marge Schott became a limited partner with the Williams brothers of Western-Southern Life Insurance Company, buying the Reds from Louis Nippert. In 1984, she bought general partnership shares from the Williams boys and on July 8, 1985 became the head honchoresse as President and Chief Operating Officer.

All these moves had to be approved by the other owners, including cantankerous Yankees owner George Steinbrenner. Commissioner Peter Ueberroth shot the approval arrow into her ample hide.

Cincinnati Enquirer - April 9, 1985

Brrrr!

Neither wind, nor sleet, nor cold... er...excuse me, that's supposed to be the mailman's creed, not the baseball commissioner attending Opening Day 1985 at Riverfront Stadium.

Doing his best to follow in the footsteps (without snowshoes) of preceding commish Boobie Kuhn, Peter Ueberroth sat in his seat coatless in a semi-blizzard.

To his credit, he didn't appear to ask Reds alcoholic owner Marge Schott to waft her boozy breath his way to warm up.

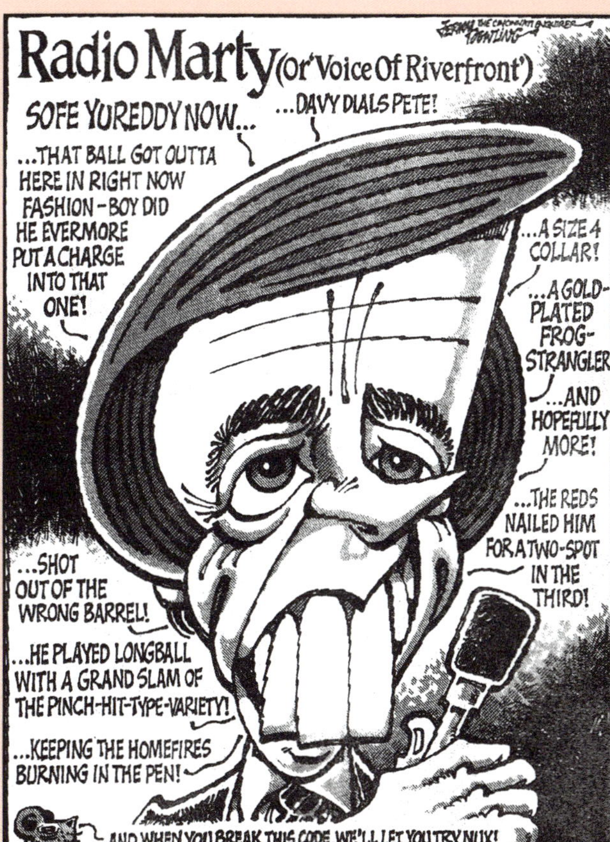

Cincinnati Enquirer - May 26, 1985

Spoken language

We should ask Brennaman if he practiced these expressions, but he's well known for them. The "This one belong to the Reds" was certainly used so often that he should have used a tape recording of it to save the wear and tear on his vocal chords!

Bienvenido!

With Pete Rose and Tony Perez returning as Big Red Machine alumni, only Joe Morgan remained AWOL.

Cincinnati Enquirer - June 2, 1985

Cincinnati Enquirer - June 8, 1985

Nickels and dimes!

Cost cutting was Marge Schott's driven obsession. Everything she did operating both her car dealership and the Reds illustrated her penurious ways.

She said that she didn't mind spending money, she just didn't like wasting it — on things like scouts ("all they do is watch ball games") and the farm system. She eliminated the fireworks, claiming ignorance as to why they were detonated (after wins and home runs, Marge), until Krogers' decided to pay that cost. She took home dining room scraps to her dogs. She forced employees to buy left over day old donuts.

Marge inherited a general manager designate in Bill Bergesch but for poor Bill, it was just that — the owner crying poor!

In spite of the financial restraints, Bergesch set out to patch a few holes, acquiring pitchers Bill Gullickson and John Denny, outfielder Max Venable, infielder Buddy Bell and most importantly, catcher Bo Diaz to fill the void left behind the plate left by retired Johnny Bench.

Chained command

Faced with the prospect of replacing Bob Howsam, Marge was left with a Howsam assistant, Bill Bergesch. But he was a man reserved enough that she could dominate him. One thing was for certain — any general manager would be treated like a dog! Bergesch at least immediately attempted to improve the team's chemistry.

Cincinnati Enquirer - June 30, 1985

Cincinnati Enquirer - July 21, 1985

Cincinnati Enquirer - September 20, 1985

Trophy time

When Mario Soto wasn't battling other players, he was at war with gophers, as in the baseball varmints.

Mario also had problems with some of the writers. Every year, the local chapter of the Baseball Writers Association of America voted on the Reds Most Valuable Player and Most Valuable Pitcher. The late Bill Ford was in charge of ordering the trophies to be presented to the winners. Mario won both. Bill, being thoughtful, combined Soto's brass (are you kidding? brass?) into one larger trophy. Was Mario happy about this? Absolutely not! He wanted two.

Cincinnati Enquirer -February 2, 1986

Head mechanic

Marge owned a Buick car dealership as well as the Reds, or should we say, as poorly as the Reds. Like the baseball gods, the auto lords didn't want her running that dealership after her husband died and she inherited the business.

She took them to court and won.

Schott operated both the same way. Cheap as possible. We went through this earlier in the book, but here's a cartoon poking fun of her saving the letters B-U-C-K from her car.

Cincinnati Enquirer - December 29, 1985

Ink stained pooch

Unbeknownst to Marge Schott, twenty game winner Tom Browning along with Bengals quarterback Ken Anderson, did a commercial for a Cincinnati Chevrolet dealership. Tom didn't realize that in addition to owning a Buick dealership, she also owned a competing Chevy one.

This became front page news, and Marge blamed the local press for leaking a story that she and Tom went at it. Dog Schottzie had to be the source as it was always snooping around her office.

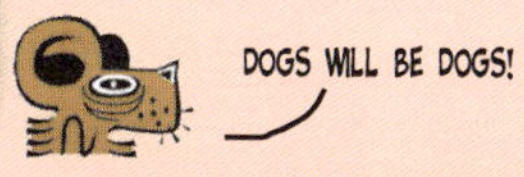

1986

Rose's bouquet!

Cincinnati Enquirer - April 7, 1986

This paper sculpture was the cover of 1986's Opening Day special edition, depicting Pete's starting rotation of Tom Browning, Mario Soto, John Denny and Bill Gullickson.

Schloshed!

Cincinnati Enquirer - April 8, 1986

Marge had a habit of calling the *Enquirer* late at night, after downing a few, demanding in her slurring speech that editorial cartoonist Jim Borgman and 'that sports guy' both be fired. For some reason, she didn't like being portrayed the way she was.

April showers

Much needed power was now being supplied by huge right fielder Dave Parker.

Dave was lathering up on National League pitchers, sending them to early showers.

Cincinnati Enquirer - April 20, 1986

Third base brawl

Eric Davis filled the July fight card all by himself with several bouts.

Some of the preliminary contests were the outfield fences, which he was assaulting regularly. He then easily took care of the bases.

The main event which people still talk about, was with former Red Ray Knight, then a third baseman for the New York Mets. As Davis slid into third, he had his face washed with Knight's glove, hockey fight style. Eric and Ray then went from exchanging angry glares to swapping serious punches. A fifteen minute brawl ensued.

700 pound umpire Eric Gregg was at third base when that skirmish broke out and his sumo-like arms restrained Davis.

Cincinnati Enquirer - July 27, 1986

Pre-Leno 'Jaws"

Cincinnati Enquirer - August 17, 1986

Grouping similar situations was the style of this series called 'Pen-Pourri' and this time it was 'noted jaws' of the sports world.

Even though George Foster was in New York by 1986, he had to be a prominent member of this collection of jaws. Not only did Yahtzee have the big lower mandible, but he jawed his way out of the Gotham at the end of the season.

Golfer Greg Norman's jaws were as hard to beat as his golf game was.

Cincinnati Bell

Cincinnati Enquirer - August 24, 1986

Son of outfielder Gus Bell, of the power laden Reds teams of the 50s, Buddy Bell came to the team in 1985, after being with the Texas Rangers for a long time.

Buddy answered the call to the hot corner, and dialed up some fine offensive numbers.

Wagging Wagner!

As the dog days of 1986 wound down, the Reds were still chasing the rabbit called the Houston Astros on the National League West dog track.

Former General Manager Dick Wagner was now the boss of the Houston gang and he had his pack leading.

After beating the Reds twice at home, the Astros came into Cincinnati and swept a three game series to mount a ten game lead. They virtually slammed the doggie door on the Reds as far as catching them in 1986 was concerned.

There were to be no treats for Schottzie to snack on this year.

The Astros, as always, didn't go any further than the division, dropping the league title to the New York Mets in six games.

Cincinnati Enquirer - September 18, 1986

1987

Early Expo splashdown

The fireworks went off early on Opening day 1987. The Reds exploded for nine fourth inning runs on the way to an 11-5 triumph. The Montreal Expos became space junk as Terry Francona, Barry Larkin and Eric Davis blasted rockets for the locals.

Cincinnati Enquirer - April 7, 1987

Cincinnati Enquirer -May 17, 1987

Grilled and drilled!

Pitchers got seriously burned when Eric Davis was on fire in early 1987. The Reds center fielder was really cooking, and the opposing hurlers were his tasty dish.

Eric actually primed the fire the previous year with 27 homers and in an injury limited '87 season, still fired up 37 of those Big Red Smokies.

Cincinnati Enquirer - June 14, 1987

Tuning up

For some reason, Tom Browning, who won twenty games as a rookie, suddenly stopped spinning out winning songs and was sent to Nashville to be rediscovered. It turned out he had been writing 'hurt' songs, resulting in the wrong kind of hits. When he returned to Cincinnati, so did his sweet ballads.

Only three?

Cincinnati Enquirer - June 14, 1987,

The Enquirer published a special souvenir section showing baseball's All-Time All-Star players at each position, plus the manager. Naturally, the Big Red Machine dominated this group, with Johnny Bench being the catcher, Sparky Anderson the manager and Pete Rose the all-around player. This just goes to illustrate how great that team actually was!

APPARENTLY I MISSED THE CUT!

Cincinnati Enquirer - September 6, 1987

Meddling Marge

Marge Schott insisted in sticking her nose, fingers, and whatever else into all aspects of team operation. Because she was the owner, she was certain that she had enough baseball smarts to run everything.

By hiring front office underlings, she had handy people to lay the blame on when things went wrong, which was often.

1988 Upstairs umpiring

Cincinnati Enquirer - September 18, 1988

Reds radio announcers Marty Brennaman and Joe Nuxhall were good at their job — announcing the action on the field. They also thought they were authorities on umpiring.

One instance where they went too far denouncing umpire Dave Pallone got them a reprimand from Commissioner Bart Giamatti. The incident where the broadcast duo took over the umpiring themselves was when Pete Rose shoved the umpire.

Marty and Joe took Pete's side on the air, inciting a mini-riot.

Cincinnati Enquirer - February 14, 1988

The Cook server

Eric Davis was coming off a career season in 1987, and had ordered his fine culinary 1988 selection.

He was dining in style, while his date, owner Marge Schott, was left to eat leftovers.

New general manager Murray Cook was the waiter delivering the gourmet meal, whipped up in the kitchen.

Marge was stuck with the tab, much to her chagrin.

Cost of that particular meal rose from $330,000 to $899,000 in one year. Even without a tip, Schott found that bill tough to swallow.

Cincinnati Enquirer - June 26, 1988

Goggle eyed!

Getting his chance to play regularly when incumbent third baseman Buddy Bell was injured, rookie Chris "Spuds" Sabo started hitting and running almost immediately. The nickname came from his manager Pete Rose, who claimed Sabo resembled the Spuds McKenzie dog of Bud Light beer commercial fame. This "Spuds" however, was never accused of dogging it on the field, noted for 'running until he's out!' notoriety.

Cincinnati Enquirer - July 10, 1988

As if tossing a perfect game gem a couple months later was enough, Tom Browning became the streak (as in the losing kind) stopper. He was dependable enough to wind up with an 18-5 won-loss record for the year. He had been only 2-3 when the fire began.

Cincinnati Enquirer - August 23, 1987

Not for this bird!

Not your typical empty nester, Reds General Manager Bill Bergesch, sat on the available chick nest late in the 1987 season, hoping to hatch a pitcher of quality.

Unfortunately, the poaching that occurred wasn't his own egg, but San Francisco Giants poacher Al Rosen, who stealthily skulked away with aging big bird Rick Reuschel from Pittsburgh.

The Reds then pulled a Humpty Dumpty act, and failed to win the division title, finishing second to the Giants.

This broken egg led mother hen Marge to push Bergesch out of the nest.

Cincinnati Enquirer - October 9, 1988

Team overboard!

These two captains of the 1988 Big Red Boat combined for 41 wins. Right handed Danny Jackson tossed 23 of those victories and lefty Tom Browning added 18. This total was more than any other pitching duo in the majors that season.

After these two, there weren't many other valuable sailors on the crew.

Only new deckhand Jose Rijo, with 13 wins, was of much help swabbing the deck. Closer John Franco was next with six triumphs.

Cincinnati Enquirer - November 6, 1988

Six eyes!

Reds rookie third baseman Chris Sabo instantly became notable for his choice of eyewear.

His choice of prescription goggles landed him a LensCrafters sponsorship deal.

Perhaps a stronger prescription would have prevented him from being thrown out on the bases so often, but the lenses didn't hurt his vision at the plate. He seemed to see the pitches well enough to smash quite a few home runs.

Kareem Abdul Jabbar and Eric Dickerson also were well known for wearing goggles while playing.

To be a Hall of Fame voter, a baseball beat writer, columnist or cartoonist must have covered the sport for at least ten years. There is also a two year wait to become a member of the BBWAA (Baseball Writers Association of America).

This cartoonist became eligible in 1971 and has faithfully voted every year since 1981, even after retiring several years ago.

A committee presents a list on which the voters then consider. It is difficult to distill that list down to the point of players deserving election. Borderline players always miss my cut.

Each year I wind up voting for only two or three. As many as ten can be voted on. It requires 75% of the writers votes to be elected. Bench received 96%.

I had no problem letting the readers know my vote in 1988, as shown in this drawing.

A check mark for Johnny Bench!

Cincinnati Enquirer - December 25, 1988

1989 One more win!

The 1989 version of the Big Red Machine wasn't quite an ambulance, so there was no need for famed chaser Stan Chesley of the Beverly Hills Supper Club fire fame to pursue this case.

After winning 23 games in 1988, pitcher Danny Jackson figured to win one more, and he accomplished that by emerging victorious in his arbitration case. It was the only arbitration case that off season.

After fellow pitcher Tom Browning settled earlier without going to arbitration, Jackson won his case and was awarded a $1,150,000 salary for 1989.

Cincinnati Enquirer - April 2, 1989

Cincinnati Enquirer - January 29, 1989

A win's a win!

Dodgers pitcher Orel Hershiser (1988 Cy Young winner with a 23-8 record), came down with the flu and wasn't able to start for the Dodgers on Opening Day.

Replacement Tim Belcher lost to Reds Danny Jackson in a sloppily played game, 6-4. The teams combined to commit five errors and there were 4 unearned runs.

1989 was a season clouded by internal squabbles and the investigations of Pete Rose and Marge Schott.

WHERE CAN I HIDE?

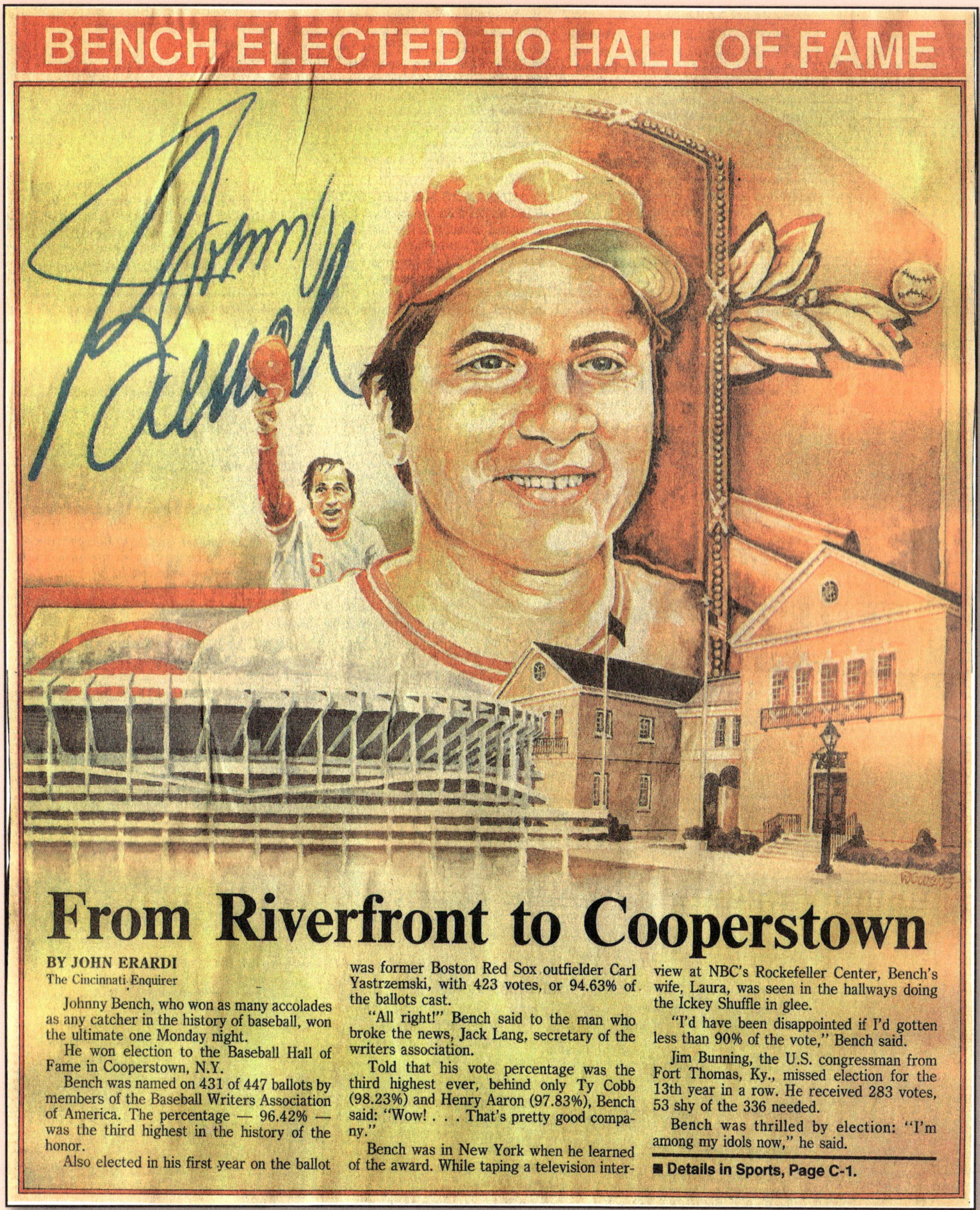

BENCH ELECTED TO HALL OF FAME

Johnny Bench

From Riverfront to Cooperstown

BY JOHN ERARDI
The Cincinnati Enquirer

Johnny Bench, who won as many accolades as any catcher in the history of baseball, won the ultimate one Monday night.

He won election to the Baseball Hall of Fame in Cooperstown, N.Y.

Bench was named on 431 of 447 ballots by members of the Baseball Writers Association of America. The percentage — 96.42% — was the third highest in the history of the honor.

Also elected in his first year on the ballot was former Boston Red Sox outfielder Carl Yastrzemski, with 423 votes, or 94.63% of the ballots cast.

"All right!" Bench said to the man who broke the news, Jack Lang, secretary of the writers association.

Told that his vote percentage was the third highest ever, behind only Ty Cobb (98.23%) and Henry Aaron (97.83%), Bench said: "Wow! . . . That's pretty good company."

Bench was in New York when he learned of the award. While taping a television interview at NBC's Rockefeller Center, Bench's wife, Laura, was seen in the hallways doing the Ickey Shuffle in glee.

"I'd have been disappointed if I'd gotten less than 90% of the vote," Bench said.

Jim Bunning, the U.S. congressman from Fort Thomas, Ky., missed election for the 13th year in a row. He received 283 votes, 53 shy of the 336 needed.

Bench was thrilled by election: "I'm among my idols now," he said.

■ Details in Sports, Page C-1.

Cincinnati Enquirer - January 10, 1989

Nothing I can write here can top the story above which was written by *Enquirer* reporter John Erardi. It was an honor to be assigned this front page illustration to run with Johnny's election story.

The reproduction you see here is scanned from the actual newspaper page. The original art which was sent to *The Enquirer's* production facility somehow never made it back to the graphics department downtown. One of the workers over there, obviously a Bench fan, has it on display at their home. Enjoy!

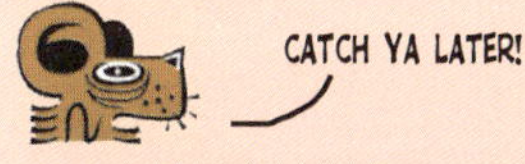

 One of a kind

When Jose Rijo took the mound to pitch, you never knew what to expect, and this cartoon depicts some of the things he did with regularity. His teammates clipped this cartoon and showed it around the dressing room.

When a batter lined one right at the pitcher, a base hit was usually the result. The exception was Rijo who, on his follow through, thrusted his glove behind has back and snatched the ball, and the surprised hitter was out.

Jose wasn't the greatest hitter, but when he was on base, he performed a super Pete Rose imitation, diving into bases.

With all these surprising acts, Jose was a true entertainer. A fan favorite.

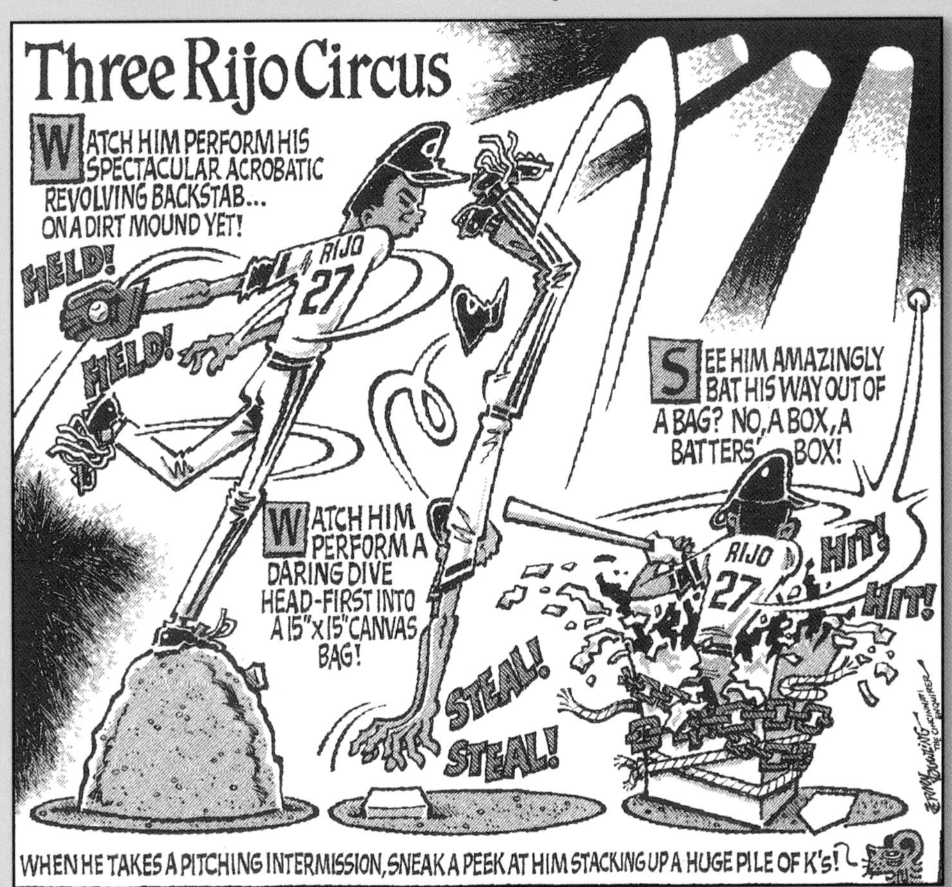

Cincinnati Enquirer - May 21, 1989

Big John!

Almost all the umpires stayed across the Ohio river at the Drawbridge Inn when assigned to Reds games. Not John McSherry. The Terrace Hilton hotel in downtown Cincinnati had a corner suite reserved for the big guy during every series he worked at Riverfront Stadium.

After games, McSherry ate a late meal of ribs at his favorite little restaurant, and later met his usual gang of friends, this author included. He regaled us with hilarious stories, made funnier with his deep Bronx accented voice and spicy language.

John knew he could trust us not to repeat some of those tales.

McSherry collapsed and died on the field on Opening Day 1996. I was supposed to meet him the next day.

Cincinnati Enquirer - May 28, 1989

H-e--r--e-s Johnny!

Cincinnati Enquirer - July 23, 1989

What a twosome!
The 1989 Hall of fame class was Johnny Bench and Boston Red Sox great Carl Yastrzemski!
It would be hard to elect two more deserving ballplayers to the baseball Hall of Fame than these two.

Fuggitit!

The Reds of 1989 were a total embarrassment, from the investigations of Pete Rose and Marge Schott, to the silly mistakes on the field.

Lack of communication, concentration and fundamentals, along with injuries combined to make it a year best forgotten.

Cincinnati Enquirer - July 30, 1989

Later or sooner

General Manager Murray Cook had been canned by Marge Schott. He was replaced by Bob Quinn, a branch of a famed baseball family tree, whose grandfather had been the owner/ general manager of several big league franchises and his father the GM with the Boston/Atlanta Braves. Quinn now had the task of inking the reluctant Eric Davis, getting new manager Lou Piniella the outfielder in the process.

His 1989 contract had been for $1,350,000.

Davis decided to take it easy in the off season. Taking his sweet old time and claiming to be unhappy with what he termed the Reds "attitude" in contact talks, Davis was trying to force a trade.

Finally, in January 1990, Davis signed a three year deal for $9,300,000.

Seems it was worth the wait.

Cincinnati Enquirer - October 22, 1989

Cincinnati Enquirer - November 26, 1989

Replacement kicks

Apparently Reds owner Marge Schott thought she had signed with the Bengals the way she practiced her kicking.

First it was interim manager Tommy Helms getting the boot, then first base coach Lee May. This was Marge's house cleaning.

Helms and May had both returned to the Reds years after the trade with Houston that brought Hall of Fame second baseman Joe Morgan to the Reds.

Tommy was serving his second stint as manager, filling in during the Pete Rose suspensions.

Schottzie the dog stayed on, and Marge didn't worry about house cleaning for that beast, she simply assigned the task of cleaning up the office hallways to her new general manager, Bob Quinn.

Lotta bull!

A few mad bulls in the Reds stockyard escaped to find what they considered greener pastures, aka more money.

The only bull that might be missed would be closer John Franco, but as it turned out, he wasn't.

The other two, pitcher Jeff Reardon was ready to be put out to pasture anyway as he was no longer a stud, while third baseman bull Nick Esasky never did perform his Cincinnati duties as promised.

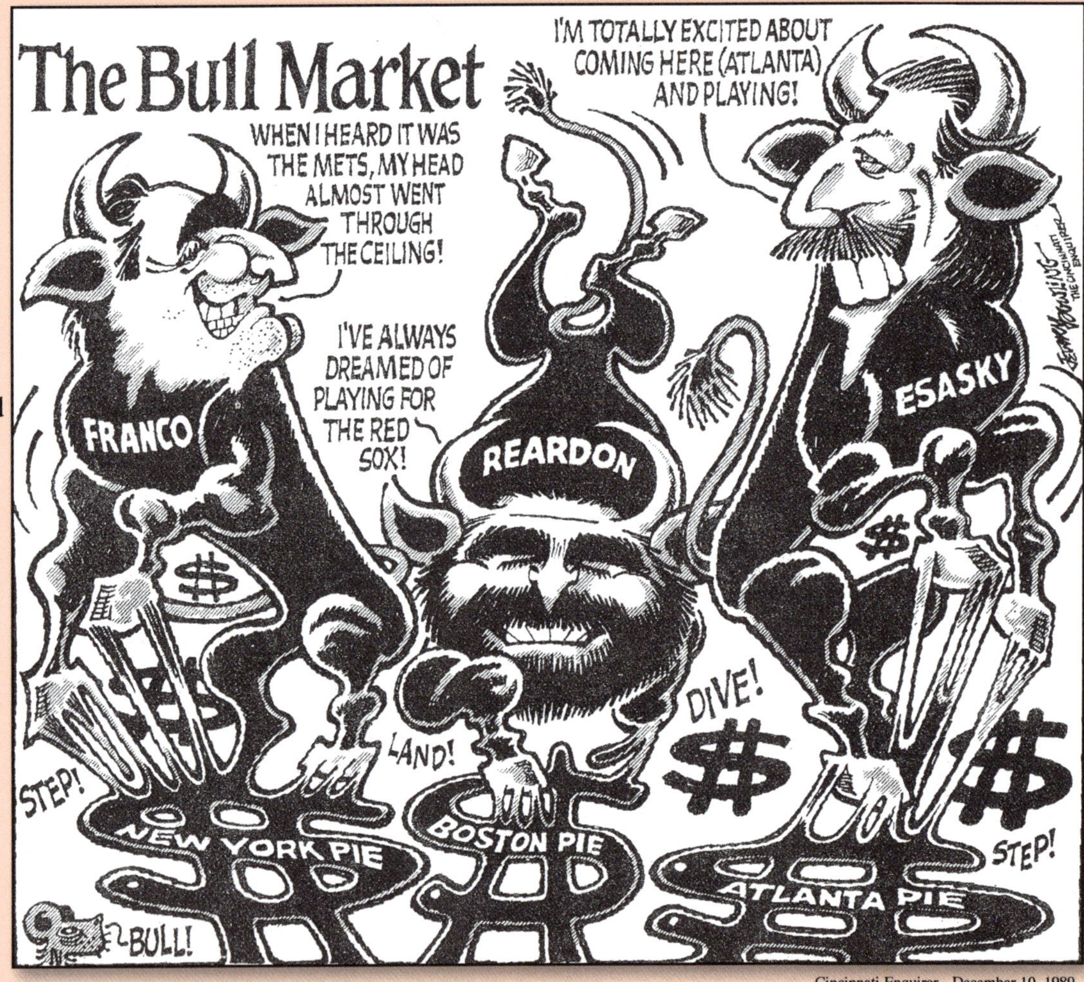

Cincinnati Enquirer - December 10, 1989

Little Joe-Big Man!

Cincinnati Enquirer - January 10, 1990

One of the key drivers of the Big Red Machine was little Joe Morgan. Joe probably gets tired of being referred to as 'little' and in truth he was anything but that. He was huge!

Obtained by Trader Bob Howsam in the November 1971 trade with the Houston Astros, Morgan came to an already good Reds team along with center fielder Cesar Geronimo, ace pitcher Jack Billingham, third baseman Dennis Menke, and utility player Ed Armbrister. The Reds gave up power hitting first baseman Lee May, all-star second baseman Tommy Helms, and outfielder Jimmy Stewart.

By having Pete Rose lead off, with Ken Griffey and Joe batting right behind him, there were usually 'ducks on the pond' for the power guys Tony Perez, Johnny Bench and George Foster to drive them safely to dry land at home plate.

The homers that went to Houston with Lee May were easily replaced by Morgan, who for a 5'7" player, had amazing power to go with his speed. He wound up smashing 152 long runs for the Big Red Machine, while May hit 147 during his time with the Reds.

Kahn's/Hillshire Farm meat packing company issued this souvenir medallion on August 5, 1990, commemorating Morgan's election to the Hall of Fame.

The drawing above was copied for the medal.

Big Red Bus

The Big Red Machine was a shuttle bus from Cincinnati to Cooperstown. Joe Morgan was the 1990 passenger, joining teammate Johnny Bench at the Hall of Fame.

First baseman Tony Perez would arrive a few years later. His luggage apparently was lost for a few years until the voters finally found it in 2000 and delivered him and his bags.

Sparky Anderson used his senior citizen pass to ride on the shuttle with Tony and entered the Hall the same year.

Dave Concepcion's admission ticket had an expiration date and he missed the bus. There is a good possibility that the Veterans Committee will issue him a new one soon.

Cincinnati Enquirer - January 14, 1990

Pete Rose though, has been thrown under the bus by Commissioner Bud "Rubbermouth" Selig.

Cincinnati Enquirer - March 25, 1990

Late arrival

Opening day 1990 was set back a week because of a labor dispute with the players, resulting in an owners lockout. We won't go into details about that, but it caused the Reds to open the season on the road. They were already in first place with six straight wins, the beginning of a wire-to-wire first place season.

They finally held an alleged home Opening Day on April 17, featuring the traditional Findlay Market parade. It was also new manager Lou Piniella's home debut.

If the season had been canceled, like the National Hockey League did in 2005, it would have alienated the fans even more, who were still miffed from the most recent stoppage in 1985.

Apparently not learning much, the baseball gods actually did cancel a post season, including the World Series, in 1994.

Three's a good company!

Most teams have one dependable closer (a specialist who enters the game, usually in the bottom of the ninth inning to protect a small lead). Not the 1990 Reds. They had three, count'em, three! They quickly established themselves as 'The Nasty Boys'.

Righthander Rob Dibble was huge — 6'4" of nastiness. With enough wildness to keep batters from digging in, combined with blazing speed, he struck out 136 batters in 98 innings. He destroyed more than hitters – chairs lockers and even the managers were victims of his nastiness.

Then were the lefties. The nuttiest was Randy Myers. He wasn't goofy on the mound, but wore army camouflage clothes and packed knives and assorted weapons. Norm Charlton was the lefty knockdown scholar who studied ways to intimidate the opposing players, including Dodgers catcher Mike Scioscia.

Cincinnati Enquirer - May 13, 1990

Cincinnati Enquirer - June 3, 1990

Warm up, sit down!

Long time Reds closer John Franco, in his first appearance back in Cincinnati as a New York Met, was in the bullpen hoping to enter the game and close his former team.

He never got the chance, although he was able to observe first hand two of his replacements. It was strikeout time for Reds Rob Dibble and Randy Myers, who fanned the side to end the game.

Lipzip!

Randy Myers was the closer on the 1990 Reds team, a role Rob Dibble figured he should have, and he complained openly.

Not happy being a set up man, Rob wasn't acting exactly like a 'team' guy, being a disruptive force on their successful run to the National League title.

Myers finished 59 of 66 appearances while Dibble did manage to close 29 games with 11 saves. Norm Charlton finished 13, but was also used as a starter – 16 times. Dibble never started a game – just fights!

Cincinnati Enquirer - July 1, 1990

Cincinnati Enquirer - July 8, 1990

Stars not out

Chris Sabo motored the Big Red Crew to the 1990 All-Star game in Chicago's Wrigley Field.

Reds representatives, cruising along with Sabo were a bunch of pitchers beginning with starter Jack Armstrong and the Nasty Boys, Randy Myers and Rob Dibble. Shortstop Barry Larkin was also in the boat.

The Reds stalwarts must have saved themselves for the regular season because none of them did anything and the National League lost 2-0, an unusually low score for Wrigley Field, a joint noted for slugfests.

Cincinnati Enquirer - August 5, 1990

There isn't much more to say about how important Joe Morgan was to The Big Red Machine. His speed, power, fielding and leadership throughout his career made him a lock for membership in the Hall of Fame. He was voted in in 1990. *The Enquirer* had two eligible voters, this book's author, and veteran writer Bill Ford, both of whom voted for Morgan.

SLID RIGHT IN!

Cincinnati Enquirer - July 22, 1990

Dirt upon dirt

When George 'The Boss' Steinbrenner passed away in 2010, old buddy/foe/employee Lou Piniella had nothing but nice things to say about their relationship.

Thing were different in 1990 when Lou was the manager of the Big Red Machine. The Boss threatened to sell information linking Piniella with extortionist Howie Spira regarding Lou's betting habits. Meanwhile, George's Yankees were at the bottom of their division, almost thirty games under .500, on the way to finishing last for the first time in 24 years.

Steinbrenner himself was getting into big time trouble, and a week after this cartoon ran, Commissioner Fay Vincent banned him for life for paying the shady Spira $40,000 to dig up Dirt on Yankee outfielder Dave Winfield.

Steinbrenner's 'lifetime ban' was only three years!

Co-tenant circus

The Reds, for a good part of the 1990 season, thought they were playing another sport since a lot of what happened on the ball field strangely looked like it was stolen from the Bengals play book.

Rob Dibble would have been the guy to dump Gatorade on somebody, although not in celebration. Norm Charlton used Dodger catcher Mike Scioscia as a tackling dummy. Chris Sabo waved at popups ala a fair catch. Paul O'Neill tossed helmets, bats, coolers, chairs, and gloves like Ken Anderson threw footballs. Lou Piniella's play calling was questionable.

Even the umpires had a problem calling fair or foul as if the foul poles were goalposts. All very confusing.

Cincinnati Enquirer - August 19, 1990

Cincinnati Enquirer - August 26, 1990

Big Red Tank job

The Reds started the 1990 season hotter than a two dollar pistol, or a firecracker and other assorted cliches and then they cooled off. And how!

They were 58-32 after ninety games, twenty six games over .500. They then played six under the rest of the season, beginning with 8 straight losses on the west coast. This laid fears that this was the real team, and the start was a Big Red Fluke. It was a tank job in the waiting.

The huge lead allowed them to limp home with the division title. It was thought that they wouldn't last long in the playoffs.

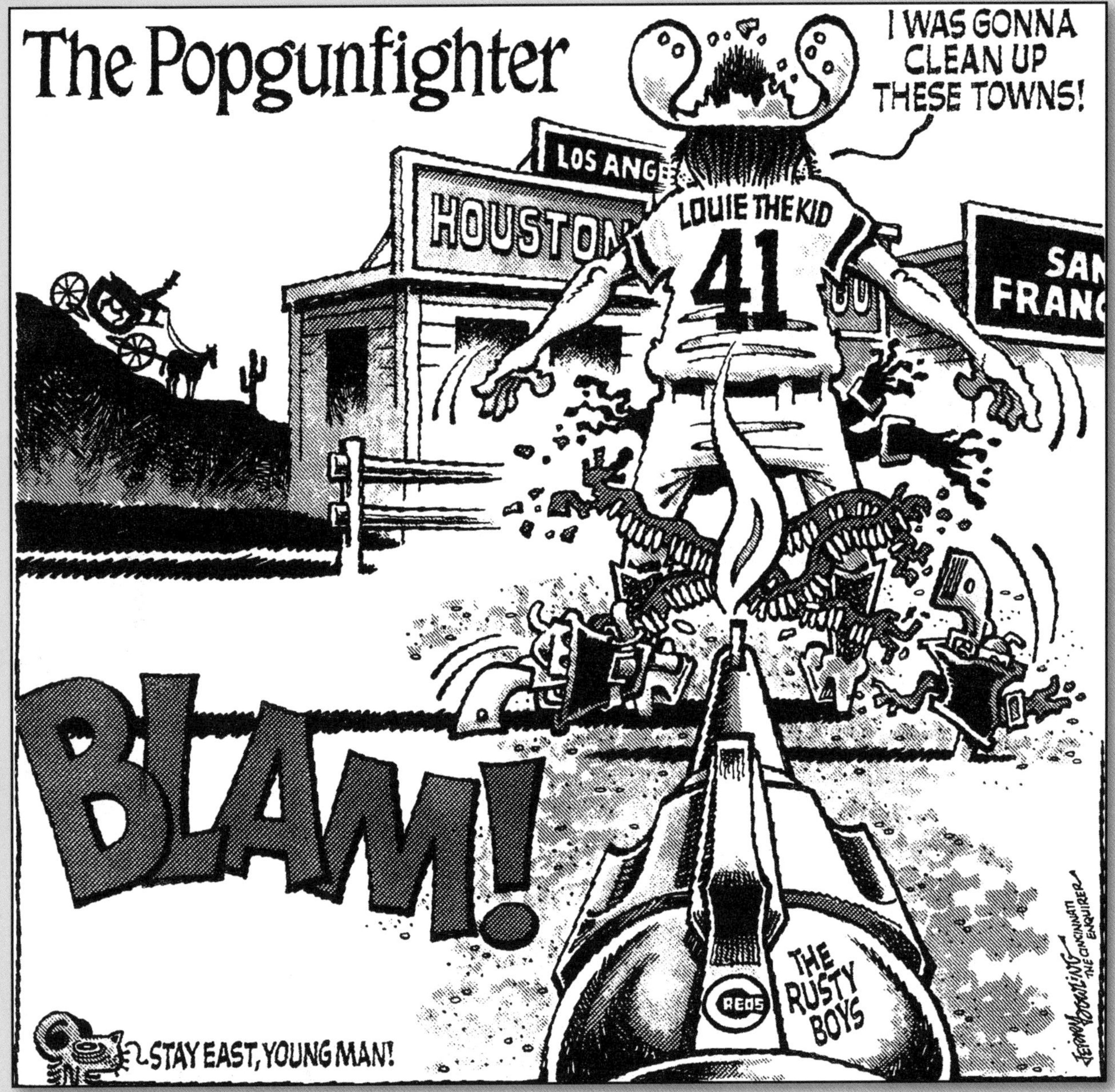

The Popgunfighter

I WAS GONNA CLEAN UP THESE TOWNS!

LOS ANGE

HOUSTON

SAN FRANC

LOUIE THE KID

41

BLAM!

THE RUSTY BOYS

REDS

STAY EAST, YOUNG MAN!

Cincinnati Enquirer - September 23, 1990

Almost shot!

Those dreaded trips west almost did the Reds in yet again. For some reason, it's very difficult for this mid-west squad to emerge victorious from the journey to Los Angeles, San Francisco and San Diego. Fortunately, the 1990 squad had built enough of a cushion to safely return still in first place. Whew!

Voodoo

Mister Red felt like a pin cushion stuck with voodoo needles as Todd Benzinger, Jose Rijo, Tom Browning and Ron Oester were trying to avoid the curse of blown leads.

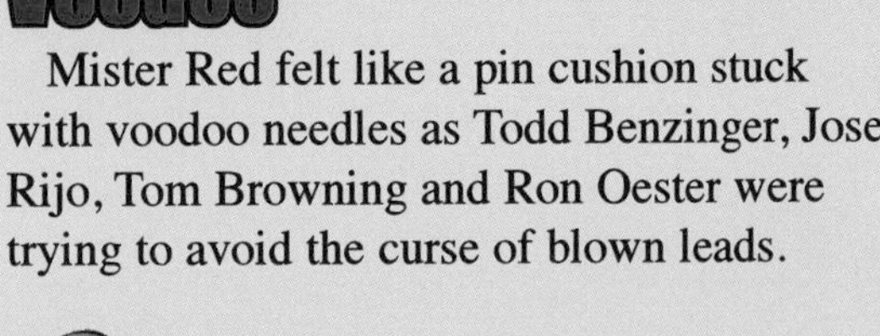

Cincinnati Enquirer - October 1, 1990

Take Me out of the Ballpark!

For whatever reason, I wasn't assigned to cover the 1990 playoffs and World Series as I had in 1970, 1972, 1975 and 1976. To ease my disappointment, I did manage to talk the powers that be to allow me to draw a cartoon to run each day of the post season games. As it turned out, it was probably easier to do it this way.

Trying to be current on deadline was a huge challenge, and many times I had to get several versions ready to publish, depending on the outcome of that day's game.

Here are the first two, and you'll find the rest of them on succeeding pages.

By the way, this entire series of originals is now at the Reds Hall of Fame, where they are displayed periodically.

My way, Jose!

Cincinnati Enquirer - October 4, 1990

Who else but ace right hander Jose Rijo would be the Reds pick as the first game playoff starter at Riverfront Stadium? With a 14-8 record and an earned run average of 2.70, he was the logical choice. Pirates starter was Bob Walk, with a record of only 7-5.

The Reds jumped out to a 3-0 lead in the first inning, but the Pirates pecked away, eventually looting the Big Red Machine, 4-3. Rijo was long gone at the end, and lefty Norm Charlton took the loss.

Logic would indicate that Walk, with an ordinary won-loss record, should be overmatched by Rijo, but logic was illogical in this case.

Way back Drabek!

Cincinnati Enquirer - October 5, 1990

The second game of the series, also at Riverfront, saw the Pirates Doug Drabek with his 22-6 record, get the call to face the Reds Tom Browning, 15-9.

The Reds again scored in the first inning, but only added one more run later. It was in the fifth inning and proved to be enough, breaking up a pitchers duel to win, 2-1. Browning got the win, Drabek the loss with a save going to one of the Nasty Boys, Randy Myers.

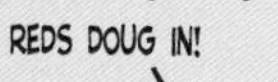

The National League championship series now moved up the Ohio River to Pittsburgh's Three Rivers Stadium. Would three rivers be better than one? We'll see! With two days between games 2 and 3, to accommodate travel (the travel must have been by a towboat with barges to traverse all of 291 miles between the two cities), the best of seven series was to resume October 9th.

These two cartoons were done ahead of time so I just used what had happened in Cincinnati as themes.

Singin' slingers!

Cincinnati Enquirer - October 6, 1990

Because we tried to run a cartoon each day during the playoffs, this one was drawn during the two day break in the series, so it's sort of a generic concept.

The Reds had two of the Nasty Boys, plus Tom Browning on the mound stage to sling a sad song (apologies to Merle Haggard) to the Pirates. The Pittsburgh nine wasn't going to record a hit this day.

Paul O'Neill wanted to let his bat do the singing, with one smash hit after another.

For those who are wondering why Dirty Rat said "Hum babies!", it was a take off on the motto "Humm baby!" used by Giants manager Roger Craig, who in 1986 for some obscure reason, thought it was appropriate to apply to a third string catcher of his, Brad Gulden.

Target practice!

Cincinnati Enquirer - October 8, 1990

Another cartoon drawn ahead of time, because of deadlines at the paper, this one simply depicted what we might expect from the explosive bat of Eric Davis, he of the high shoes.

The star center fielder had his usual injury shortened season in 1990, but still blasted 24 homers and drove home 86 runs.

And I never missed a chance to show the immense girth of several National League umpires.

Back to baseball? Remember that? It's not known if the teams traveled by boat, plane, bicycle, train or bus to get from Cincinnati to Pittsburgh. They could have walked.

Half dozen sweet runs

Cincinnati Enquirer - October 9, 1990

Finally back to playing, after the first ever scheduled two off days in a playoff series, second baseman Mariano Duncan drove in four runs including a three run shot, in the Reds 6-3 victory in Game 3.

The win gave Cincinnati the series lead. Billy Hatcher had opened the scoring with a two run homer in the second inning and Mariano took care of the rest of the Pirates' Duncan dunkin'.

Pittsburgh's Three Rivers Stadium now had a shipwreck to deal with.

Give me your mouth!

Cincinnati Enquirer - October 10, 1990

Nasty Boy Norm Charlton carried his nastiness a little further, ripping the home fans perceived lack of support. In the playoffs yet.

Charlton, usually known for his pitching, had some memorable hitting also, most notable the flattening of Dodger catcher Mike Scioscia earlier in the season.

For a team that went wire-to-wire to claim the West Division title, its loyal fans would expect it to roll over the opposing Pittsburgh Pirates, who actually had a better won-loss record during the season. Any thoughts of that happening were dispelled by this series. It wound up being a hard fought six game win for the Reds, but four of those games were decided by only one run. The Bucs were tough!

Smell something?

Cincinnati Enquirer - October 11, 1990

Lou Piniella had his Big Reds Iron ready to finish taking the Pirates to the cleaners in Game 5 of the playoffs. Pittsburgh ace starter Doug Drabek had other ideas.

This was a rematch with the second game starters with Tom Browning on the hill for the Reds and the results were reversed with Drabek emerging the winner.

The Pirates were charred, but not quite ready for the season ending smoldering trash pile.

Buried for good!

Cincinnati Enquirer - October 12, 1990

Game six - a night game - an early drawing because of those dreaded deadlines. Unlike a reporter whose stories can be changed, although grudgingly, at the last minute, cartoons can't be.

This wasn't a prediction, but I'll claim it.

Jackson was noted for dragging his left foot into the dirt on the mound during his follow through, so naturally he might as well dig a hole in which to bury the Pirates. As it turned out – he did – allowing just one run while reliever Norm Charlton got the win, 2-1.

The Oakland A's were huge favorites to whip the Reds in the 1990 World Series, having racked up 103 victories while winning their division by nine games over the Chicago White Sox, and sweeping the Boston Red Sox in four to cop the league title. So dominant was their pitching, led by Dave Stewart, that the Bosox scored exactly one run in each game.

The Reds beat the Pittsburgh Pirates in six, but didn't exactly blow them away. Even though they went wire-to-wire, they played barely .500 baseball the latter part of the season. Many thought they backed into the National League crown and would be no match for the A's

Twenty five wheeler!

Cincinnati Enquirer - October 13, 1990

Country singer Dave Dudley recorded several hit songs but his signature tune was "Six days on the road".

Since the 1990 version of the Big Red Machine dispatched the Pirates in six games (actually taking nine days because of scheduling), I decided that the fat lady could sing the song.

It wasn't Roseanne Barr or even Marge Schott. Those two could meet the obesity category, but neither could sing, as Barr once proved by disgracing the National Anthem.

The first leg of the trip was only down the road to Cincinnati for the first two games of the World Series. Again, with television ruling the schedule, this short journey took four days.

Early riser

Cincinnati Enquirer - October 15, 1990

With the first game of the 1990 World Series still a day away, this cartoon simply depicted Reds skipper Lou Piniella rising to meet the challenge of taking on the American League champion Oakland A's.

Eccentric A's owner Charlie Finley wasn't around this time, having sold the team in 1981.

American League champion Oakland A's of 1990 were a power hitting gang, featuring Mark McGwire and Jose Conseco, known as the Bash brothers. They hit 39 and 37 respectively. Also doing considerable bashing were the Hendersons, Dave and Rickey, who added 48 more long balls to the team total. As if that wasn't enough power, the A's also had two powerful pitchers, Dave Stewart and Bob Welch, winning 49 games between them.

The underdog Reds power duo was Chris Sabo with 25 home runs and Eric Davis with 24. Their top pitchers were Tom Browning who won 15 games, and Jose Rijo with 24. The A's won 103 games in the regular season, while the Reds emerged victorious with a mere 91. Who would you pick?

Stop, thief!

Cincinnati Enquirer - October 16, 1990

Speedster/master thief extraordinaire Rickey Henderson had returned to the A's after several years with the New York Yankees. He was salivating at the thought of adding Reds bases to his huge collection of loot.

I did this pre-series cartoon showing Reds manager Lou Piniella, who had practiced and perfected the art of tossing bases, devising a plan to stop Henderson's thievery. Whether it worked or not, we'll see.

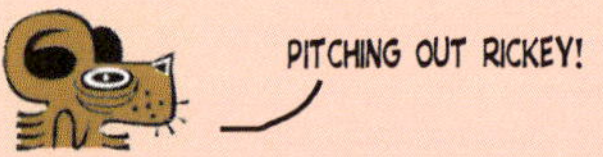

Big relief!

Cincinnati Enquirer - October 17, 1990

H. Dubya the first was supposed to toss the first pitch of game 2, but a 'budget crisis' forced him to cancel, and first lady Barb pinch pitched for him. Ever thoughtful Marge Schott had a seat saved for her back in the stands, along with commissioner Fay Vincent.

Dog loving Schott had her look-a-like mutt Shottzie (a creative name if there ever was one) in attendance and she invited first dog Millie to help with the pooping. "What a bunch of crap!" Millie barked as she decided to stay home too.

Riverfront Stadium was all set to host it's fifth World Series. This 1990 season saw the Oakland A's as the American League foe for the second time, having defeated the baby Big Red Machine in seven games way back in 1972. The A's of that era were indeed a dynasty, finishing first in their division five consecutive years and winning the World Championship three straight times, beginning with that 1972 triumph over the Reds.

The 1990 A's were at the end of another streak of three straight World Series appearances, winning one, in 1989 over the San Francisco Giants, a series best remembered by an earthquake which resulted in a ten day interruption in the series.

Derailed!

Cincinnati Enquirer - October 18, 1990

The upstart Big Red Machine upended the heavily favored Oakland A's of Tony "The Genius" LaRussa in both of the first two games in Cincinnati, 7-0 and 5-4.

Those upsets caused genius boy to wonder what went wrong on his tracks to the World Championship. The rails were obviously laid wrong and his A's were sent in a different, unplanned direction.

Somehow, the A's made it back to Oakland, hoping conductor LaRussa would punch the right tickets and switch them back to the right track.

Bubbly Billygum

Cincinnati Enquirer - October 19, 1990

Reds outfielder Billy Hatcher's career can be summed up by his amazing performance in the 1990 World Series. He hit .519, going 14 for 27 at the plate. At one point during the series, he had seven straight hits, which prompted this cartoon.

Even so, he wasn't even voted the series Most Valuable Player, with that award going to pitcher Jose Rijo.

DOWNED THE HATCH!

Most baseball people consider the '75-'76 teams to be the real Big Red Machine, but the grinders on this 1990 squad don't accept that concept. While the '70s team had so many huge stars — you know — a slew of Hall of Famers and a couple more who should be in Cooperstown, the 1990 team had no player who would be considered Hall quality other than possibly outfielder Paul O'Neill who hasn't yet acquired the necessary 75% of the votes, and likely won't. Schottzie the dog? – NO!

Unscheduled time out!

Cincinnati Enquirer - October 20, 1990

Tom Browning was slated to start game 3 in Oakland. While he was sitting on the bench during game 2, his wife Debbie went into labor. Tom left the dugout, and went with her to the hospital. Manager Piniella frantically searched for him in case he was needed to pitch if the game went into extra innings. A message even went over the radio and TV broadcasts to tell him to get back to the park. Browning ignored the message, stayed with his wife and a baby son entered the humanity game.

Chris Sabo had a couple presents for the new father, double wrapped in home run paper.

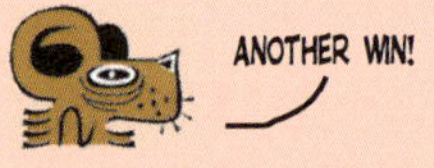

Jose can't you see?

Cincinnati Enquirer - October 21, 1990

Bash brother Jose Canseco was pretty much an unbasher in this series — sore back, sore finger, sore head, sore .091 batting average. He got himself benched by LaRussa for sloppy, indifferent play, but pinch hit with one out in the 9th inning of the final game. He weakly bashed a grounder to Chris Sabo at third and was out. One out later, a foul pop up to first baseman Todd Benzinger ended the game and the Big Red Guys were World Champions of 1990.

Square Schott!

The drawing shown here is the last one of the series you've seen on the previous few pages. I actually was complimentary to Marge, which was more than a challenge, and basically a cartoon type lie. General manager Bob Quinn, who was once told to clean up a hallway from dog poop, generally managed to find the parts to build the 1990 model of the machine.

Marge, even penurious in most ways, still gets the credit for spending the money to bring in the players Bob Quinn needed to assemble the squad. Quinn, in my mind the best general manager the team has had since Bob Howsam, did the job with crafty trades and drafts, although working with an extremely limited budget.

It's too bad that Marge couldn't even remember names other than "Honey", calling one player "catcher" Oliver.

Cincinnati Enquirer - October 22, 1990

Photo by Gary Landers, Cincinnati Enquirer - March 25, 2010

In 2004, Reds owner Carl Lindner ordered CEO John Allen to get going on building a Hall of Fame and Museum, to be located next to the spanking new Great American Ball Park. With baseball historian and author Greg Rhodes, the executive director, the Hall opened in September 2004. Special exhibits occur there periodically and the set of drawings referred to earlier had a display of its own, lining a hallway.

This cartoon of Marge popped up again, part of a 2010 show honoring the 1990 team.

High (usually) and mighty

One of Marge's many flighty gaffes referred to the troops in the "far" east. Obviously she knew nothing about geography, MapQuest? Google maps? Radar? Sonar? AAA? — none of those would have helped her, and if GPS had been around, it would have cost her too much. AA? Maybe!

During Game 4 of the World Series in Oakland, Eric Davis lacerated a kidney diving for a ball and spent eleven days in the hospital recovering. Miserly Marge even refused to pay for his flight back to Cincinnati.

I tied these incidents together and aired out this cartoon.

Cincinnati Enquirer - November 4, 1990

The Cincinnati Enquirer
Monday, April 8, 1991

BASEBALL '91

SEATTLE MARINERS
TEXAS
TORON BLUE J
San Fra GIANT
OAKLAND ATHLETICS
San D go PADR
NEW YORK YANKEES
ST. OUIS CAR INALS
Minnesota TWINS
burgh RATES
MILWAUKEE BREWERS
iladelphia PHILLIES
Kansas City ROYALS
New York METS
TROIT GERS
Montreal EXPOS
C and IN ANS
Los Angeles DODGERS
CHI AGO WHI E SOX
HOUSTON ASTROS
CALIFOR IA ANGELS
CINCINNATI REDS
BOSTON RED SOX
CHICAGO CUBS

WORLD CHAMPIONS

MANAGER
LOU PINIELLA

1990, the last of the three great Big Red Machines!

Cincinnati Enquirer - April 8, 1991

Afterword

By Bob Quinn, General Manager, Big Red 1990 Champions

MAGICALLY UNBELIEVABLE
These two words best describe the 1990 season !!!

The 1990 World Champion Cincinnati Reds were the first National League team to go "Wire-To-Wire"... That is, they were never out of first place from Opening Day thru' the final day of the Championship season!!!

The 1990 Reds were truly a "blue collar" bunch. Starters Jose Rijo and Tom Browning anchored the starting rotation, complimented by Jack Armstrong and Scott Scudder. And, let's not forget that reliever – Norm Charlton – started several crucial games down the stretch as well. The starters were complemented by the "Nasty Boys" out of the bullpen. When the '90 Reds took a lead into the sixth inning, it was all over. Manager Lou Piniella called upon the "Nasty Boys".

The everyday player line-up was equally blue collar, led by "Mr. Steady" – Barry Larkin. Of course, every player in the starting line-up made significant contributions to this CHAMPIONSHIP effort. Players coming off the bench were also terrific.

Lou Piniella's unrelenting determination to winning was never lost on his players. Lou and the members of his coaching staff turned the "Blue Collar" boys into World Champs!!! Despite losing eight (8) straight games on a late season western road trip, the team re-bounded – a reflection of Lou's intensity and the teams' dedication to WINNING!!!

Simply put - The 1990 World Champion Cincinnati Reds were: "MAGICALLY UNBELIEVABLE"!!!

-Bob Quinn

Other Books From Edgecliff Press

I Thought Pigs Could Fly!

Americans Revisited, Vol. 1

Drawing The Big Red Machine

The Collected Old Curmudgeon

Staglieno: Art of the Marble Carver

Sucking it up: American Soldiers in 2008

Drawing Super Wars: The Early Years of Bengal Football

Cincinnati's Findlay Market - A Photographic Journey, Past & Present

Managing Nonprofit (& for Profit) Organizations: Tips, Tools and Tactics

Pre-Victorian Homes Drawing Pete

Right, Angels!

Body Of Work

Your Best Shot

Point Of View

Anything Goes

From Edgecliff Kids

When Big Artists Were Little Kids

When More Big Artists Were Little Kids

When Big Architects Were Little Kids

Alena and the Favorite Thing

Cincinnati Trips with Kids

Hobo Finds a Home

Cliffie's Life Lessons

Paragon & Jubiliee

The Curious Moog

CPSIA information can be obtained
at www.ICGtesting.com
Printed in the USA
LVIW021141230912
299766LV00007B